# The Life and Adventures of Bert

Anderson Graham

Bert the Bear

Published by Bert the Bear in 2022
Written by Jean Graham/Ross Graham
Cover design by Radu Muresan
Typesetting and interior design by Claire Wingfield Literary Consultancy
Illustrations by John Heim
Photograph design by Muhammad Junaid Afzal

# The Life and Adventures of Bert

2010–2020

Dedicated to the women in my life
Mum and Gran
Who loved me more than any gentleman could wish to be loved
Let's do it all over again one day.
Love Bert x

To call him a dog hardly seems to do him justice, though, in as much as he had four legs, a tail, and (very rarely) barked, I admit he was, to all outward appearances. But to those of us who knew him well, he was the perfect gentleman.

— Hermione Granger

Bert. Our best friend. Forever.

2010–2020.

# Contents


Preface xi

1. Fate 1
Chapter One: Fate 10
2. New Beginnings 24
Chapter Two: New Beginnings 36
3. A Mother's Love 61
Chapter Three: A Mother's Love 67
4. New Home. New Adventures 84
Chapter Four: New Home. New Adventures 93
5. An Older Gentleman 111
Chapter Five: An Older Gentleman 119
6. Goodbye For Now 144
Chapter Six: Goodbye for Now 146
7. Legacy 160
Chapter Seven: Legacy 165
Epilogue 192

Notes 195
Acknowledgments 197

# Preface

To write it, it took three months;
To conceive it, three minutes;
To collect the data in it – all my life.

— F. Scott Fitzgerald (The Author's Apology, 1920; *This Side of Paradise*)

This is not only a story of a dog but the story of me; of us. To get to the heart of a person, go by way of the dog, and vice versa. I began writing down Bert's life story for my therapeutic process. Remembering became cathartic. Little memories, which, at the time, hardly seemed worth remembering, became precious. Remembering returned the smiles and replaced the pain.

It all started when my mother gave me a special birthday present. She wrote Bert's life story in verse. Reading it to me around the dining table brought laughs, smiles, and tears. I immediately mentioned that I would have to print it as a book, a forever keepsake. We kept adding to the poem as new memories were rekindled in our minds. The whole process helped with the grieving; sharing and discussing memories we each had. The next stage was writing down the in-depth details of the verses, the finer aspects of our memories.

The book has grown to be a truly collective endeavour. I discussed my passion project with friends on Twitter and had Bert's followers requesting to read the story. For me to make it available for others to enjoy. These friends supported the project by sharing their favourite memories of Bert. They gave me advice when I did not know which direction to turn and provided feedback to allow me to tell the story in an accessible way for all.

I wrote this story because my love for Bert is beyond words, and I believe he deserves a memorial and tribute worthy of his life. I hope to portray him as he was; not a 'Superdog', but just a super dog.

Many adventures have come and gone, and many years have passed. And maybe this is not exactly the way it was, but it is precisely how I remember it.

This is a story I had to tell.

A life I had to share.

# 1. Fate

I wanted to say thank you for saving me that night
You changed my life forever, made everything just right
I'd say that it was fate, and it was meant to be
That you would be the one who came to rescue me.

Dodging all that traffic was certainly not fun
So, when you tried to catch me, I didn't try to run
Felt sure that I'd be safe, and you'd be kind to me
And what a wise decision that turned out to be!

You saw that I was skinny – my ribs were showing through
My nose was cut and tender. I was pretty smelly too!
But soon, all that would change, and I would start to thrive
My coat all soft and shiny; my eyes would come alive.

That first night I remember, I was sleeping in the hall
It was warm and cosy, with lots of room to sprawl
When it came to walkies, I wasn't filled with hope
You didn't have a lead, just a tatty skipping rope!

What a sorry sight we were, walking down the street
All the time, I'm praying, my owners we won't meet
A scruffy, skinny lab who looked just like a stray
I'm surprised that no one phoned the SSPCA.[1]

We went to meet your folks, but I think it's fair to say
I wasn't feeling confident that I was here to stay
So, I had to take my chance to stock up on some food
But with hindsight, I admit, that was really rather rude!!

Your dad put down his roll – I could smell the lovely ham
My eyes were wide as saucers, but I managed to stay calm
But then he turned around, and I couldn't quite resist
Just hoping all the time, his lunch would not be missed!!

I still remember clearly; well, how could I forget?
The smell and the temptation of a big garlic baguette
No matter if it's frozen; still tasted pretty good
Remember, I'm a lab, so I REALLY like my food!

The strange thing I remember was that nobody got MAD!
They didn't reprimand me or tell me I was bad
Then, I knew for certain, no longer would I roam
'Scout' was gone forever, and 'Bert' had found his home.

And that's where I met Alfie, the other golden boy
A lovely gentle lab, your brother's pride and joy
I wasn't very sure he'd let me share his space
But thankfully, he did, as I really love this place.

We were always VERY different, especially up the field
I would take it slowly, and his pace would be revealed
A hundred miles per hour, catching balls up in the air
I was like the tortoise, and he was like the hare.

A trip to 'Captain Dugwash' to take the 'smells' away
And when they heard my story, they pampered me all day
I was head to toe in bubbles – treated like a king
Washed and scrubbed my ears; they didn't miss a thing.

But oh, it was so lovely to feel so fresh and clean
My coat, now soft as silk; the best it's ever been
Now smelling of deodorant with no more matted tufts
I'd surely win 1st prize if you'd taken me to Crufts!

I really must be dreaming; two square meals a day!
And what was even better, I got treats along the way
I couldn't quite believe it; my life had turned around
I only started living on the day that I was found.

Not once, from that day forward, did I ever misbehave
For I knew that I was loved and forever I'd be safe
The memories were fading of that former life I'd led
Waiting by the bakers in the hope that I'd be fed.

**Anderson Graham**

I'd started to imagine our 'Happy Ever After'
When a message on your phone, all my dreams would shatter
"Hello. We've found the owner. The dog can go back home
He does not need to wander; he has no need to roam."

Already we had bonded, I was meant to be with you
I watched you shed some tears, more than just a few
Surely, we can fix this. There has to be a way
That you can change her mind, and I'm allowed to stay.

I never will forget what might be our 'final walk'
Last moments spent together, seconds ticking on the clock
This would not be easy. I can see that in your eyes
You'll have to hand me over and say our last goodbyes.

As we headed to the park, my heart was full of fear
I knew that you were shaking when my owner did appear
Please don't take me back. I love this life I've found
I didn't leave your side, paws firmly on the ground.

You told her that you'd found me and how we'd spent our days
She saw how much you loved me. Your words so full of praise
I didn't move a muscle, my heart so full of dread
Until I heard those words that my 'former owner' said.

'I think that you should keep him. You clearly have a bond
He's looking very good, and of you, he's really fond'
I really can't believe it; heart missed a beat or two
Did I really hear her say I can come and live with you?

And as we leave the park, my paws don't touch the ground
The fastest I have moved; don't even turn around
It's farewell to my old life – the new one will be great
We're meant to be together. I told you it was fate!

I saw your hands were shaking as you lifted up your phone
To spread the brilliant news; you'd no longer be alone
So much jubilation, you grinned from cheek to cheek
How your life has changed, in shorter than a week.

There are moments in your life that stand out from the rest
Such happiness and joy, they truly are the best
And that was one such moment, the moment that I knew
We'd never be apart, and I'll spend my life with you.

# Chapter One: Fate

This is the story of Bert. A dog just like countless others, yet, extraordinary.

On the first night of my Easter holidays, April 28th, 2013, I decided to go 'back home' and visit friends in Scotland's most vibrant city – Glasgow. Driving home around midnight, out of the corner of my eye and through the darkness of the night, my car's full beam lights caught a glimpse of a dog wandering onto the motorway from the upcoming slip road. From that moment, that brief look, my world became a much brighter place.

He was a 'braw' looking dog; handsome, muscular, and beautifully made with a great disposition. His head was broad, his paws huge, but he was skin and bones. His nose was cut from scavenging in bins, and ribs clearly showed through his matted, golden fur coat. I thought he was an old soul – his face thin, his eyes tired. He was living an utterly self-reliant lifestyle. Roaming at large and accustomed to independence to survive. However, what I remember most about his appearance that night was his ear-to-ear smile, with front teeth like miniature stepping stones of a causeway. He had not been living a 'dog's life' and was glad to be found.

Dogs take their lives as they find them, but they live it best with the purpose of pleasing others.

However, he was a streetwise puppy and wouldn't allow me to coax him into my car away from potential danger. So, off came my belt, placed loosely around his neck, and we walked, slowly plodding, until we got somewhere safe to stay the night. A friend was refurbishing a flat nearby and let us stay the evening. On the walk back, we were stopped by a taxi driver – "That's the dog that's been dodging traffic all night."

How quickly he adopted an admiring and trusting approach. Despite his apparent initial defiance and reluctance, he was willing to abandon his most primal instincts and trust my guidance without question. The poor outcast of society blinked up with his brown, soulful eyes, pleading as if to say, 'take me with you'.

I did not save him that night. I did what any humane and decent person would do when witnessing an animal in need and living in hopeless misery. Animals have a unique way of pulling our heartstrings. Even Napoleon, in *The Memorial of Saint Helena*, tells of walking through a field of the dead after a battle when he witnessed a dog loyally beside its master's body. Observing the canine licking the dead man's face, he stated, 'No incident, on any of my battlefields, ever produced so deep an impression on me'.[1]

I had never owned a dog before. Growing up, I had always loved dogs, but I can only remember a handful of dogs throughout the entirety of my childhood.

There was a wonderful friend of my mother, Margaret, who had the most humongous Irish Wolfhound called Roy. Irish Wolfhounds are the tallest breed of dogs in the world, but I think Roy may have been the tallest dog of the tallest breed. A giant, but a big, friendly giant. He looked like he deserved to be sitting at the side of an ancient King's throne. Grand, regal – almost medieval and mythical in appearance. I would lie on the floor and colour in some drawings whilst Roy snuggled beside me. He dwarfed me; every so often, his tongue could cover my whole face with a slobbery swish lick. However, the real reason I remember Roy was that he could fly. Sitting on the sofa, as my mum and Margaret had a chinwag, we looked up to witness four legs sprawled out, fully stretched just below the ceiling, flying above us to land in the middle of the living room floor. Roy did not see the point of running down the whole staircase when he could just leap from the middle of the stairs, over the sofa and any unsuspecting visitors, for the ultimate shortcut. I think it was his party trick. For anyone lucky enough to have grown up watching the 1984 fantasy classic, *The Neverending Story*, Roy was Falcor. It made a young boy very happy.

Later, I learned Roy was a wandering stray dog found on Margaret's doorstep. At the time, he was a tiny puppy with wiry grey scruffy hair. When all attempts to find his owner failed, they made the visitor a permanent resident in their home. I loved this story. It seemed like fate. However, I am not entirely convinced they knew he would grow to be seven feet tall.

That first night, I took photos of the lost dog curiously searching the hallways. They were dark and grainy but showed his nose cut and long-drawn face. I look at these photographs now, and despite the poor quality, I cherish them as it demonstrates how much he flourished from that day forward.

It was late in a tiny Scottish village far from civilisation – the kind of place where no shops are open past sunset. I had no dog food, but the starving, stray dog happily gulped down what was in the cupboard – baked beans. The following morning let's just say the old children's rhyme was correct. He was not house-trained, and the baked beans must have had too much fibre!

This prompted our lifelong morning routine. "Want to go for a walk?" Did I have a lead? No. However, being a Physical Education teacher, we always have random equipment in the boot of our cars, and I found an old cotton skipping rope. That will do, and we went for a walk around the local village. Let's explore.

He was happy. I was happy. From day one, that boy had my heartstrings. So much of life is complicated and convoluted, but this was simple and pure.

I contacted the police to leave information and went to the closest vet to check for a microchip. Both were unsuccessful. However, on our walk, we got some clues when we met locals who knew him – "that's the dog who's been stealing the rolls from the bakery".

Every dog needs a name to be called when out for walkies. Finding a name that suits a dog's appearance is vital. I envisaged myself having to recall him back, regaining control in a busy park in the presence of well-behaved dogs on proper leads. Funny dog names are not so amusing when desperately shouting a dog's name, embarrassed or stressed, and being blatantly ignored. It should be short and sharp. Syllables kept to a minimum and sound reasonable in every situation. He already had an ancient soul, so I chose a name fitting for an old Scottish gentleman – Bert.

Now that I had gained his trust, we hopped into the car and headed to my family home, where my brother's dog, Alfie, lived. He had plenty of leads and dog food to share. Both dogs were Golden Labradors and were of a similar age. However, seeing them together, the differences in the type of Labrador were noticeable. The new boy was shorter, legs closer to the ground, and of a stockier frame. His head was broader, muzzle shorter, and much larger bear-like paws. They also had VERY different personalities. Despite this, they were always happy in each other's company. This was the beginning of a lifetime bromance – even though Bert peed all over Alfie's food bowl on his first appearance as if to say, 'There's a new guy in town.'

Most of my experiences with dogs were with the Golden Labradors in my family circle. There is always that one dog who turns us into a 'dog person'. That dog which lets a young child know that dogs can be the most loving, trustworthy, and loyal of friends. For me, that dog was Glen. Like Bert, he was an old-fashioned, British golden Labrador with a square head, hazelnut brown eyes, and a permanent dangling, salivating tongue. Glen lived with my Aunt Sheila and Uncle Dougie and was known for his mellow and sweet nature.

Everyone loved Glen. He loved the postman and waste collectors. Whining to get out to welcome them on their morning routes, he would run to the gate to say his greetings, receive a pat on the head (or ten) and a black bin bag to return home – all in his day's work.

I loved visiting their house to play football. Glen was always the goalkeeper. My brother and I could play for hours, bringing carnage to my aunt's home, trying to score past the golden goalie who would use his speedy reflex reactions and large jaws to stop any shot.

Glen introduced me to a Labrador's powers of persuasion. Knowing the location of Glen's treat cupboard, I would sneak into the kitchen and get out the jar of dog-friendly chocolate buttons. I opened the clear glass jar, gave Glen one, and then helped myself to one. One for you, one for me. He was so gentle with his mouth. Uncle Dougie used to let me give Glen treats after we returned from walks around the streets and down to the local park. He convincingly told me Glen used to be a special police dog. Whilst walking around the park, Dougie would point at mounds of dirt and say that was where Glen buried a bad guy that he caught. Sadly, I was much older than I would rather admit before I realised this was not the case. Glen was too gentle and kind. Most importantly, he was my friend.

I was in Primary Five, around nine years old, when I came

home to get organised for school football training with some friends when Sheila called to tell us that Glen had died. That was the first time in my life that I truly understood and experienced loss. I slammed the living room door, and the glass vibrated, almost to the point of shattering, before crying uncontrollably. Glen was my first heartache. He was a good boy and set a standard which judged all future dogs to cross my path.

It was not until I was 25 that I let my heart fall in love with a dog again. During the first week of the summer holidays in 2011, my brother visited a wedding venue when he remembered reading that puppies were for sale nearby. On his return home, my mum asked how they liked the wedding venue, and he didn't even respond to the question, instead blurting out, "We put down a deposit on a puppy." Scott picked up puppy Alfie, a golden Labrador, and I was determined to be his best friend.

I lived away from 'home' at the time, but every weekend, I would come home and go for walks with Alfie. I would take him out, babysit him, and feed him. It was my first experience of having the responsibility of looking after a dog, and I loved it. He would bite and nip me playfully with razor-sharp teeth, steal toilet paper like the Andrex puppy, and attempt to come into the house with mud-caked paws. Still, he was the most adorable little furball. He could do no wrong. Alfie was obsessed with licking my eyes, and the face was not good enough. If I shut my eyes, he would stop. Alfie was desperately trying to wash the windows to the soul to see my character; desperate to kiss it or clean it. Alfie always wanted to be on top of you. Proximity was not enough. On top, his jaggy elbows were usually placed right into your chest and ribcage, but we all know the rules; you are not allowed to move a dog when they are comfortable.

Alfie had two main methods of entertainment – water and balls. Alfie was gone if he got a whiff of a chance to head off into a water source. Out of sight, seemingly out of hearing range, before reappearing soaked to the bones. He was an athletic swimmer. He had the technique, endurance, and speed. Labradors were bred historically as water dogs, expected to catch fish or pull in fishing nets in freezing cold, rough seas. Alfie would have made his ancestors proud. However, there was an occasion when out walking alongside a loch when Alfie put his stamina to the test. He quickly slipped into the water, and we noticed he was swimming further and further out into the loch without any intention of returning. His destination was a ball, or lots of balls. With the course set up for a boat event, there were buoys out in the loch to direct the boats, and Alfie went out to bring one back to shore. Realising his initial buoy, or ball, was steadfast and true, he moved on to the next. Then the next one. Paddling along tirelessly, Alfie surfaced with 'Limber Tail' or dead tail – occurring due to overexertion in the water. After a few days of rest and pampering, he was as right as rain.

However, he remained ball obsessed. He would love nothing

more than to go up to the 'field' to play fetch. Alfie would bark his head off when he heard the word or knew the car was driving in that direction. He had the navigational skill to know which direction the car was going and its final destination. Controlling him for those twenty yards from the car to the entrance was demanding work, pulling with the power of a team of sleigh dogs to get started. He could chase all day. He would sprint down the hill to get the bouncing ball or 'go long' and, with me playing the quarterback role, run ahead and catch the ball in mid-flight. He would plough down, full steam in the direction of the ball and would take out anyone or anything in his path. His brakes required servicing as they never appeared to work. He would side-step walk, staring at the ball, waiting for its release. He was so obsessed as a youngster; at times, it could have been argued the purpose of his existence was to chase down a tennis ball.

Alfie is a stiff boy now, older, and I know we were naïve and regret some of those games. At the time, we only knew how much fun he was having. A more relaxed ball game was played between Alfie and my mum. He would be 'goalkeeper', and she would chuck the ball a step either side of him for him to react and save the ball. A game which has continued for a lifetime.

He had fantastic discipline. When the humans frequently tired and went back inside, Alfie would sit for as long as it took at the back of the garden, just staring, waiting for someone to come back out and start throwing again. Determined or stubborn, he stuck to his guns. To this day, at the ripe old age of eleven, nothing has ever changed. He decides which of the finest cuts of meats he would like for his dinner, where and when he will go for a walk, and which of the beds will be his for the evening. Spoiled and treated like a king – but rightly so.

Anyway, back to the story.

Bert went to be washed and groomed. Under all that filth was a silky, smooth coat; gold of sunshine in his hair, which now smelled of lavender and sage. Beautiful. Next stop, we went to the pet store and got a bag of food, treats, a comfortable bed, collar, and lead – things every dog deserves. Even if it were only for a day – he would experience luxury like a much-loved pet.

In his first few days, he took every opportunity to get food in his belly and seized what he could spy. He didn't know how long this would last. My dad lost his morning breakfast roll on day one. Some lovely gammon went as well, if I remember correctly. However, it was the first meal together when the fun began. My parents cooked a spontaneous lasagne and invited my brother over for our first family meal. Some garlic baguettes were found in the freezer and needed to be left out to defrost. When it came time to cook the baguettes – they were nowhere to be seen! Naïvely left within reach on the kitchen worktop, the hungry Labrador could not help himself and somehow managed to crunch, munch and chew through two hard, frozen baguettes. As Oscar Wilde would say, he could resist everything except temptation[2]. He was lucky he did not live in the Eighteenth Century, or he would have been hauled up in front of a judge on an animal trial. Although Bert could plead his innocence as there was no physical evidence of this ever happening. Still, anyone in the room, anyone within a radius of a few miles, was in no doubt where the garlic goods had gone – anytime he opened his mouth. Despite a bulging belly full of frozen delights, he crudely watched us eat every single mouthful with mounting interest throughout that meal. The length of saliva drooling from both sides of his mouth increased with every bite. Our plates were closely guarded by his stubborn optimism and an enigmatic gaze every meal we ate that weekend.

Food was a crucial element in Bert's life. Food was, and is, vitally important to a dog, but especially a Labrador. Even more so to a starving stray Labrador. He was in a survival mode of eating to live and not living to eat. That came later. The taste was secondary. In fact, I often doubted if he had ever tasted his meals when he inhaled them with such speed and vigour.

We went on many walks around the street that weekend. Bert's nose was stuck to the ground, refusing to stop until every inch was examined. He was on a mission to sniff every corner of the unfamiliar environment.

He could not get enough ear rubs, physical contact, and being admired or coddled by everyone he met. It was clear that this dog was perpetually lacking in love and affection. There were no doubts he liked it, and there were no doubts he needed it. Dogs let you know with instant, visible, or physical feedback. Seeing him content, tail wagging, made everyone happy. His love was instant and uncomplicated. He wanted love, and in return, he would vastly improve the lives of those who loved him.

Three days later, my world was turned upside down. I was notified that the owner had come forward. I was broken. I remember being in a car park sobbing uncontrollably. Somehow, I had fallen in love with this dog in such a short space of time. Within days he had become an integral part of our family. What did Bert do to earn his new status and affection? He hadn't had to do anything.

Reluctantly, we said our goodbyes, he licked the tears off my face, and we went to meet his owner.

He NEVER left my side. He was constantly underfoot, the shadow by my side. I could not speak. Explanations of what happened were given, and the story of his three-day holiday was exchanged. Then, witnessing how happy he was by my side, out of nowhere – "You should keep him."

The next part, the jubilation, is a total blur. All I remember is a man and his dog walking away together, seeing nothing but each other.

That is the story of how I found a dog, fell in love, and my world changed forever. If I had been one minute earlier – if I had been one minute later – I would never have met my best friend. That was the singular moment in my life which was the catalyst that determined the rest of my life.

Life without a dog would be immensely simpler but not nearly as fulfilling.

It was Fate.

# FIRST 24 HOURS

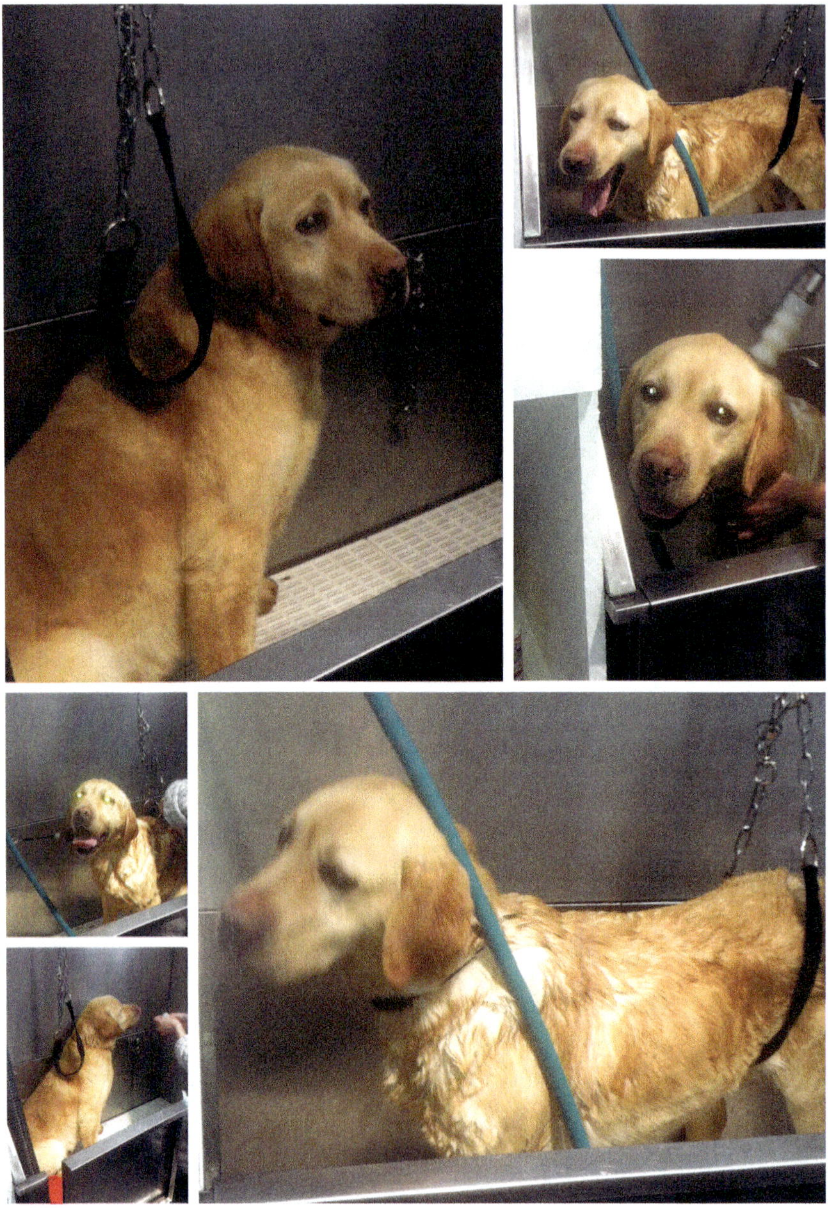

# SCRUB-A-DUB-DUB

ALFIE AND BERT

# 2. New Beginnings

You took me up to Alyth – the place which I'd call home
With hills and fields and rivers – all places I could roam
'The Den' became my favourite, with its gently running stream
I had to pinch myself to be sure it's not a dream.

Strolling by the river to a shallow spot I'd found
I'd have a little paddle then suddenly PLOP down
This became my trademark – a special gift, I'd say
Just 'plopping' in the water in my own peculiar way!

Walking round the golf course, you'd run ahead of me
Then, for some strange reason, climb up the nearest tree!
"Come on Bert and find me; it's hide and seek", you'd say
I'm embarrassed to admit – never found you to this day!

The Bluebell Woods a favourite – perhaps a weekend treat
Ambling through the woods and all the folk we'd meet
Stopped and said, "He's lovely – a credit to his breed"
I couldn't quite believe it – that was praise indeed!

Lovely morning sunshine glinting through the trees
And multitudes of bluebells swinging in the breeze
I plopped down in the middle to enjoy the perfect view
Another golden moment to be shared by me and you.

**Anderson Graham**

Some days I loved the best, the favourites in my life
Were when we took a drive to the villages of Fife
With summer sun's arrival, we'd spend a lovely day
Playing on the golden sands of Elie's Ruby Bay.

Unspoiled shores and sand dunes – a dream for all us mutts
We see the distant lighthouse as we pass the wee beach huts
Mum and dad behind me, always close at hand
Striding out together, leaving pawprints in the sand.

In younger days, when fitter, we'd explore the Coastal Trail
Setting out for Anstruther, from the harbour walls of Crail
Past St. Monans' windmill, to the boats in Pittenweem
I feel so very grateful that I got to live the dream.

ST. ANDREWS
fore!
CRAIL
EAST
NEUK
PITTENWEEN
ST. MONANS
ELIE
we love
Bert!

We'd pop into Janetta's, for St Andrews' best ice cream
You licked the top; I ate the cone – we made quite the team
Then on to the location of *Chariots of Fire*
The West Sands of St Andrews – which many do admire.

Then if we timed it right, head to golf's official home
On Sunday, when the 'Old Course' is free for all to roam
Shake my cute behind – making sure it could be seen
As we crossed the Swilcan Bridge towards the 18th green.

Your parents went to Kingsbarns on holiday each year
And we could go to visit as it was fairly near
This place was just idyllic – a doggy paradise
Rivers, fields and forest trails, everything so nice.

That's where Cousin Alfie came with us to the beach
In the sea you'd throw the ball, almost out of reach
Alfie bounded onwards, crashing through the waves
Then swimming like a fish until the ball he saves.

I would dip my toes in, a metre from the shore
Sometimes even knee high but never venture more
Plop down in the water and stare in disbelief
Surely all that effort would only give you grief?

'Labradors love water', or so they always say
That was true for Alfie; he'd swim and swim all day
I just never understood it. It all got out of hand
Just have a little paddle, then head back to dry land.

Sometimes we'd reach the beach as the tide was heading out
"Come on Bert, let's hurry," I would hear you shout
Plodding to the water took half an hour or more
A twenty-second dip, then straight back to the shore.

That never made you mad. No harsh word did you speak
Instead, it made you smile and laugh, say I was unique
All my little quirks and traits, I'd often hear you say
Made me extra special – living life Bert's way.

My bed was in the kitchen, at first, as I recall
But you and I both knew that wouldn't last at all!
And soon I made my way to your cosy bed upstairs
As now we were a team – dad and Bert the Bear!!

Remember when you caught me on the stairs one day
Looking rather guilty, I would have to say
My cover had been blown – there's no more to be said
When you were out at work, I'd be in your comfy bed!

My favourite time of all – when we cuddled up at night
You'd tell me that you loved me, and things had turned out right
"That night, we BOTH were saved", were the words you said
to me
Your life was so much better and all because of me!

I've never been so proud in all my life I'd say
As I listened to those words, that you said that day
You made me feel so special – filled my heart with joy
Thank goodness that you found me, and I became 'your boy'.

Our neighbour she was 'old school', Maisie was her name
Not one for sloppy kisses but she loved me just the same
No need for fancy cameras or high-spec door alarms
Maisie had our backs and kept us free from harm.

My first birthday living with you, a card came in the post
Although just one of many, this surprised the most
It came from Grampa Don, for his favourite gent
You and gran were shocked. It's the first he'd ever sent.

I'd visit Gran and Grampa – my home away from home
They'd take me up the field, new paths and trails to roam
Then back to fill my belly – chicken, mince or treat
My belly was expanding; no more a slim athlete.

Aunt Sheila came to visit, and I'd gently take her arm
(By now, I was an expert at turning on the charm)
Lead her to the cupboard, which stored the tasty treats
And every time – it never failed; she'd give me one to eat.

I had a little relapse just round this time
She made some buttered toast and thought it would be fine
To leave it on a table – just inches from my nose
I have no need to tell you just how that story goes!

Each morning, on a workday, we had the same routine
As you looked back up the path, my face was clearly seen
Squashed up against the glass watching as you go
Then upstairs for a kip – a boy needs his sleep, you know.

You had to find a walker, so to 'Kittywoof' I'd go
I'm amazed that Gordon took me – did he know I'd be so slow?
"Go and make some friends. You'll love it, wait and see"
But all that 'pally wally' stuff was really not for me!

The other dogs were running and jumping in the loch
I just sat bewildered – in fact, I was in shock!
All that catch and fetch and chasing round with sticks
Made me tired just watching, so I just sat transfixed!

Each night you'd see the photos of dogs all having fun
Gordon with his camera catching each and every one
Sometimes take a video, around the scene he'd pan
You'd find me in the background like the grumpiest old man!

Why waste a lovely walk running round like mad?
I much preferred to amble and stay beside my dad
Surely all those zoomies must make a boy feel ill?
The BERT way is the best way – just lie around and CHILL!

You once went to the pictures – returning late at night
I stayed at my pal Millie's and we gave you such a fright
The 'rat bait' box was open but no contents could be found
The vet said it was urgent – bring in the greedy hound!

TWO dogs were made to vomit – who's guilty? Wait and see
You looked into my eyes and knew it wasn't me
And sure enough, the verdict – I'm innocent it's true
The culprit was wee Millie, whose sick was powder blue!

You took on many challenges – raised funds for those in need
We featured in a magazine for everyone to read
Your help and motivation was 'Beatson Bert' they said
Joining you on training runs (in truth, I stayed in bed!)

Those days, two boys together, were special times for me
Spending lots of evenings in front of the TV
Both sprawled out on the floor – me right against your hip
Especially on 'fish supper' nights – I'd always get a chip.

# Chapter Two: New Beginnings

Bert's new life was one full of love.

It was split between Alyth, where I lived during the week for work, and Airdrie, where I returned to the family home each weekend.

## Alyth

Monday to Friday, Bert lived with me in my little chocolate-box farming village in rural Perthshire, Scotland. Outside our front door was a 'burn'; the lovely little stretch of water kept the locals on their toes by occasionally bursting its banks as the rain ran down the hills. It was a very small village, overlooked, in each direction, by rolling green hills. Within a few minutes' walk, we found ourselves on country paths to the golf course, frolicking through the fields, or dipping our toes in the water. It was perfect and a far cry from the world we can only imagine Bert was used to.

Before Bert arrived, my existence there was purely for work. It was a base, and Bert made it our home. He had quickly become the key ingredient to all my happiness, and every day was brighter.

We explored. New routes, new paths, new adventures.

Our favourite was a deep-sided wooded valley called The Den[1]. It was a pleasant long walk to the entrance, over a traditional stone Roman arch bridge and past an old, abandoned wood mill. It was a long-looped route, alongside the babbling brook, walking up, and down, either side of the steep, craggy banks where the burn tumbles down the hills. The tall beech trees cast much of a shadow in parts of The Den. There is certainly no shortage of leaves to be kicked come the season when the trees shed their summer coats. Kicking autumn leaves is something you never are too old to participate in, man or dog.

We reached a wooden footbridge through a narrow gorge with tall red sandstone cliffs rising on the far side of the burn. Occasionally we would stop on the bridge and play 'Poohsticks', just like Winnie-the-Pooh and Christopher Robin[2]. Bert would place his chin on the bottom rail, or his head underneath the railing, as he lay down to watch the river slip away. I would drop a stick on the upstream side of the bridge, and he would watch it slowly pass below. Sometimes Bert would saunter to retrieve it. Other times, he just let it float away and watched it disappear out of sight from his position of comfort. However, all Bert cared for was that water. It was cold, and he hopped into the shallows. It flowed into and against his joints and body like a refreshing massage. It was here Bert learned how to plop. He would remain motionless for a moment of quiet, unruffled happiness.

Our usual morning walk before work was through the fields on the outskirts of the village. Paths ran through the middle of the crops, or after harvest, just expansive fields of large, round hay bales. We would always stop to greet the horses. They appeared to trust Bert's gentle nature and approached the fence for a stroke and scratch while Bert lay on the ground and took a rest. When the hay bales appeared, this was the trigger for playing hide and seek. Whenever Bert dilly-dallied too long over a specific scent, I ran off to hide behind a hay bale and then whistled for his attention. The result was a confused dog, looking around in bemusement, checking hay bale to hay bale until he found me.

'Hide and Seek' was a game which was frequently played when he lagged on walks. My strategy was that my sudden vanishing act would create a mini panic or at least a level of confusion. Bert would drop everything. His feet would scurry to search to the end of the world for his best friend. However, often blissfully unaware, he continued plodding on, head to the ground, and sniffing the temptations left by previous guests. When he was polite enough to entertain me and play, he froze like a rabbit caught in the headlights, head up, searching in every direction. I would whistle to assist his search efforts and give him a sense of direction. This failed. Bert had a terrible awareness of where sounds came from and scampered off the wrong way. To avoid him disappearing into the horizon, I would have to leap out and run after him, shouting to get his attention. Perhaps he outsmarted me, a ploy to stop all the shenanigans.

One day when Alfie joined us for the weekend, I thought I would play whilst we explored a dense woodland. It was a terrible idea which nearly ended catastrophically. Sensing my opportunity, I found a large oak tree and scurried up to hide. Whistling to coax them, I expected to watch two yellows searching endlessly below. Oh, it would be hilarious! However, Alfie's eyes locked onto me, and before I could climb down, he began the ascent upwards. Clambering up, branch by branch, suddenly he lost adhesion and fell. It unfolded in slow motion. He helplessly and hopelessly clutched at thin air with his paws before falling, landing on his back on the grass below. In total shock and panic, I have never been so relieved to see a dog wag his tail.

On weekends or bright summer evenings, we would take a drive and go for a walk along the riverbank of the River Ericht, or preferably, to the bluebell woods. It was a special place for us. I took a school running club which used the woods as part of their route and wanted to share its beauty with Bert. It was peaceful and secluded. We would walk through single-track paths, past horses and cows, and into a small wood. In the summer months, the floor was awash with bluebells sweeping steadily over the hill. Smooth, bell-shaped flowers with upturned tips. The most beautiful shade of deep violet-blue. On one occasion, whilst resting, Bert sat on the edge of the path, surrounded by bluebells. The pictures we took that day remain some of my favourites of my precious boy. It was a beautiful setting for making memories.

We were only a short drive away from Scotland's East coast. Windy, cold, but always beautiful. The East Neuk of Fife played a pivotal part in my childhood, and it was always a place I felt an affinity for. Anytime the sun made an appearance, it lured me.

From the age of five to fifteen years old, every summer holiday, we went to Kingsbarns. Where we stayed, a farm cottage set in a rural paradise, was idyllic. The dogs used to love to chase, sniff, wander the paths, dip into the shallow burn and run through the plentiful cropfields. My parents often go back for weekend retreats, and we always make an appearance. Kingsbarns has one of Scotland's cleanest and prettiest golden sands, which travels to the distant blue haze where the sea meets the sky.

However, the real reason we wanted to return as children was their resident black Labrador, Brambles. He lived in the 'big house' on the farm but would make his way around the cottages every evening, hoping, and always succeeding, to get treats from as many homes as he could. Just like Glen, he was so gentle, and I spent a substantial portion of each holiday trying to coax Brambles back to our cottage for the evening. He would come in and lie down with us to watch television until the owner came round to lock up the pool, and then we would have to send Brambles back home until the following day. We were allowed to take him on walks around the fields; for that fortnight, he was ours. I got incredibly jealous when other children, from other cottages, wanted to play with MY dog. On one of our final summer trips, we were there when Brambles passed on. We got to lay stones at his graveside and say our goodbyes to our friend. I remember thinking I would never have a dog of my own and voluntarily put myself through that inevitable heartbreaking experience.

For Bert, the beach contained fresh rock pools to plod, plop and 'dook[3]'; hoping he didn't disturb any grumpy crabs. Alfie was more attracted to the crashing waves to run and dive into and through, wherever the tide may take his ball. Alfie was a true Labrador, bred with boundless energy, and had that impulse to charge into waters like his ancestors, who were a fisherman's best friend. There is a joy of the seaside humans never truly recapture as we grow old, but most dogs never lose it. Bert was an exception. He wished to gaze at the dazzle of the sand directly beneath his chin as he lay and rested.

It was only a short drive away from the world-famous St Andrews. More recently known as the town where Prince William met Kate but for the past hundred years known as the 'Home of Golf'. Despite having a population of less than twenty thousand, the small coastal town houses seven golf courses, with 230,000 rounds played each year. St Andrews is such a wonderful place to spend a day. It is quiet but has atmosphere. The town is small but grand, achievable by foot, and great for a stroll with our four-legged friends. Through the cathedral's ruins, along the cliff tops to the castle, down to the West Sands along the long stretch of golden beach.

On a Sunday, the famous Old Course, considered the oldest golf course in the world, is open and welcome to everyone – except golfers. It was a perfect space to roam freely. The closure is traced back to religious laws of the 16$^{th}$ Century regarding what people could do on the Sabbath. Historically, local fishermen took advantage and spread their nets across the fairways to mend them for their week ahead at sea. Nowadays, Sundays are taken advantage of by tourists who wish to be engulfed in the history of walking across the famous Swilcan Bridge, where all the greatest golfers have scraped their spikes. Or dog walkers exploring the vast, expansive grounds. Dogs didn't require to head to the beach to exercise on Sundays as the course contained 112 bunkers full of sand to frolic through. The bunkers originated on the Old Course when it doubled up as a home for grazing sheep. To protect themselves from strong winds whipping in from the North Sea, they burrowed holes to hide for their safety. It was decided to leave them as part of the design, and the infamously difficult pot bunkers remain to this day. Every visit to St Andrews, whether sun, rain, or gale, ended with an ice cream tub for the dogs to indulge and lick clean.

East Neuk had many beautiful seaside villages to discover along the Fife Coastal Trail. Arriving for the golden sunrise, Elie was our starting point. Bert plodded across the stretch of unspoiled white sand at his own pace. In parts, firm but smooth underfoot; in others, he was made to work for each step. Alfie barely felt the sand between his pads as he bounded and glided swiftly across the shoreline. He headed directly towards his destination with only one goal: getting wet. There were waves to chase, waves that crashed, waves to leap and waves which tumbled angrily like thunder. Alfie liked to explore the deepest waters. Beaches were not just places where lands end and seas begin, but gateways to new adventures. However, I think the sea daunted Bert. It was vast and empty. He used to enjoy gazing out into the sea from where the rolling waves rested smoothly after losing their power.

We would always stroll over to the white lighthouse on the edge of the North Sea, built over a hundred years ago to light the Isle of May just off the coast. The North Sea could be grey, choppy, forbidding but anytime we sat at the foot of the lighthouse with Bert, looking out, it appeared to shimmer with light across the vast blue reach. We would venture through the ruins of Lady's Tower with its amazing views over the bay, built in 1760 as a lavish changing room for Lady Janet Anstruther before her skinny-dipping bathe in the sea, then past the crumbling walls of both Ardross and Newark Castles, onto the village of St Monans. A tiny, picturesque fishing village with a famous zig-zag stone pier, designed as a breakwater to protect the community from the harsh North Sea, and St Monans windmill, the last remaining windmill from Fife's salt panning industry and one of the most striking images along the coastline.

On Bert's final walk on the coastal trail, this stretch was far enough for him. Exhausted in the heat, he recovered in a beer garden with gran and grandpa whilst we walked back to Elie to retrieve the car, then our boy.

During peak years, we could go further onto Pittenweem, down its steep, sea-cliff walls to the active port and only working fishing harbour in Fife. The morning fish market brought the smell of the morning catch hanging in the air. Patrolling seagulls screeched and swooped down on dropped morsels, disregarded by the fishermen amongst the lobster traps. The tides and waves were low, but the sails were high on the brightly hulled fishing vessels, jostling for position as they prepared to anchor. Bert found pleasure resting on the harbour and observing the hustle and bustle which unfolded. He was in sensory overdrive.

However, the main stop was Anstruther, home to the famous Anstruther Fish Bar. After a morning stroll, plod, and excursion along the coastal path, it felt well-earned. Surely, we had burned enough calories. A chip for me, a chip for Bert. His recognition for his efforts. I did not share my breaded fish supper, though – it was too good to share.

Still a young dog in this period, he could walk for miles and miles in his glorious, youthful prime[4]. Never fast, even in his youth, but he loved to get out, plod, sniff and wander slowly around the countryside, streets, or coastal paths. It was an expedition we took on in the sunnier months each year.

I emphasise slowly. There was a period when I became obsessed with fitness. I would go for long runs or cycle the country roads after work. However, I always cut short the sessions to get back to Bert. One day I decided to kill two birds with one stone and invite Bert to be my running sidekick. I remember constantly stopping and trying to get him to keep going, motivate or tempt him. Nope. Stubborn. I then tried attaching a long leash to his collar and coaxing him forward – that boy just demonstrated a determination and stubbornness to be admired. He firmly anchored his bum to the ground and refused to move. He only ever ran on his terms, and those terms were very infrequent. Unsurprisingly that was our first, last and only running session as a team.

In the summer months, Bert and I used to get up at the break of the day and hike up the hill which overlooked the village. Our wee hill, in our wee village, was linked to ancient folklore. It was rumoured that following the death of King Arthur, his wife Guinevere was taken to an Iron Age fort on top of the hill and savagely pulled apart by wild animals for betraying the king.

My dog and I were morning people. No matter how many times we climbed that hill or paced ourselves, that initial steep climb up the rocky trail always took some fair effort. Both man and dog absolutely knackered, shoulders moving up and down, panting heavily together after the ascent. Gazing at me with his bright brown eyes, pleading for just a moment's rest. Reaching the gentler inclines at the top, Bert came alive. He loved to run up and down the slopes. There were times I would see those large flapping ears, that determined face and those four short legs sprinting, appearing over the ridge of the dip, into my arms. Occasionally forgetting to brake and knocking me onto my back. He bounded through the long grass and heather as pheasants cackled and exploded out of the thick, surrounding gorse.

It was magical up there. It was ours. An escape. This vast space and not a single other person to be seen or heard. Moors of low scrubby and jaggy vegetation on either side of the path. Extensive covering of mosses, bracken, and shrubs; so wild and empty. Glorious riots of colours; shades of purple and yellow from the heather and gorse, sprinkled across the mounds and moors. Sometimes the hilltops were green, transitioning to gold and brown as seasons changed. Living and walking with a dog reinforces your solitude; I was more satisfied by the understanding and companionship which existed between Bert and me than any other human.

At the summit, 984ft, there was a bench. We always stopped and sat on the bench, occasionally catching the glorious sunrise lifting over the skyline. It was our moment of reflection, looking over the world below us. The world stood still, and our eyes were drawn to the far, unbroken horizon. Panoramic views which had been earned. Hills and valleys below which remained unchanged for thousands of years. I truly appreciated those moments. Man and dog. Man and best friend.

In our village was the BEST fish and chip shop. That is not an exaggeration. It won multiple awards, and it just happened to be two-hundred yards from our house. A good and bad thing. Initially, Bert got a chip or two from my Special Fish Supper after the exertion. By our final days in the village, when Bert was a well-known face, there occasionally was a surprise sausage wrapped up beside the fish supper – for the dog. This was the beginning of the end – that starving lost dog whose ribs were on show – he was gone.

I used to always lie on the floor. To eat, work or watch TV. Bert always snuggled beside me. His head rested on the edge of my food tray, as close as he could encroach without being restrained.

Or on my papers when trying to work. He just wanted attention. I was more than happy to give him that. I rarely sat on the sofa or at the dining table when I lived alone. It was my boy and me, cuddled up, snug as a bug, watching TV. I loved that. So simple, but there was so much comfort and love in those moments.

Initially, he did not seek much demonstrative affection. He would slip into the hallway to nap if there was no excitement or food to be gifted. His positioning was tactical; he could observe me and anyone walking up our lane from his vantage point. Most importantly, he would be alerted if I attempted to enter the kitchen. It was enough for him to be just out of reach but always watchful.

Our physical bond was strengthened through play. Or, more accurately, play fighting. He loved a stramash, a battle, or a brawl; but only with me[5]. Bursts of unbridled joy, 'ferocious' adrenaline and spurts of energy. He would demonstrate a mixture of the martial arts. He lunged, whirled, snarled, and gnawed. Bert remembering his Scottish roots, occasionally threw in a 'Glasgow Kiss'[6] for good measure with his rock-hard skull. Teeth baring like Cujo, clamping onto my wrist as we tussled on the ground. His teeth were on me, just enough pressure to hold but not hurt. He liked to roll on the floor. A lazy approach. Twisting and turning, side to side, like a wrestler evading being pinned. He went into a berserker rage, running down the hallway, around tables, in full zoomies mode but always bounding back for more. However, as soon as I said 'enough', he resorted to wanting belly rubs, still twisting and turning, fangs showing but eyes pasted closed. He was only ever gentle. It was our thing.

When I went to work each day, Bert was lucky enough to have two visitors until we were reunited: Gordon and Maisie.

Although Bert could confidently be left without fear of accidents or destruction, he was collected each day by Gordon, his dog walker. He was scheduled to take Bert for a one-hour walk each lunchtime. My neighbours frequently told me he could be away for several hours at a time. Bert was the last walk of the day, and Gordon loved being outside with the dogs. Always exploring new beauty spots with many other energetic dogs, Gordon walked dogs of every possible size, shape, breed, and age, but they all had a lovely temperament when they were under his control, and with each other. He was a dog whisperer. Dogs could be running freely and wild, and with one short whistle, there would be six dogs sitting on top of a stone together, awaiting their next instruction.

Gordon would send videos and photos of the dogs' adventures every evening. Bert was a character. In the group photos, all the other dogs displayed big smiles, tongues dangling and tails wagging. Bert was always the dog who looked miserable, grumpy, or sulky. In videos, the other dogs pranced, danced, chased, and wrestled. Then the video would pan round to see Bert, on his own, just looking in utter bewilderment at these other dogs and their chaotic, foolish, energetic behaviour. Initially, I was worried like a parent who witnessed their child in the school playground with no friends. However, I realised over time, that just was not Bert. He loved Gordon. He was happy. But he was just a dog who preferred his own company and doing things at his own pace. On his own terms, he was a maverick who refused to bend to social norms. Bert was never a dog who wanted or needed the attention of other dogs or people. He only wanted that small circle of a family he knew, trusted, and loved. It is all he wanted or needed.

Bert's other visitor each day was Maisie. Officially my next-door neighbour but unofficially, my guardian angel. Maisie was in her 80s and had lived in her home for over 50 years. She was the encyclopedia of everything and everyone in the village. I could not have asked for a better neighbour. She looked after me.

I was 22 years old when I moved far away from home, alone and totally naïve. My mum was always so thankful for her presence. When Bert arrived, I could go to work each day knowing he was safe. She was a one-person neighbourhood watch. Maisie would collect my mail and packages and take them to my house. Even if there was no mail, she would occasionally pop in to ensure everything was okay (and even sometimes washed the dishes I left that morning). She was never one to pet and play with dogs, rather shoosh him out the way, but Bert respected her, and she cared for Bert. However, she would never tell him that. She was old school, not one to show her feelings, but it was clear.

Leaving for work, Bert often pressed his face flush against the frosted glass of the front door and watched me, with his sad, puppy dog eyes, all the way to my car. He made me feel guilty with each step. When I returned from work, Bert would occasionally still be there, staring, and it made me feel terrible – he hasn't been there waiting all day, has he? I was assured by Maisie he had not. He just knew his routine. His timings. He knew it was walkies as soon as I was home; it was Bert time. He was ready and waiting. I was informed that he slept snuggly most of the time, but when he was awake, he sat observing throughout the day. This placid, friendly dog doubled up as an intimidating home-alarm system. To the unknown visitor who dared come to our door, they would be greeted by a giant powerful beast on hind legs, roaring from the top of his lungs. In reality, he was just desperate to say hello, with welcoming enthusiasm. Throughout the summer, the door would be opened. Bert's chin rested on the step and the sun shone on his face. Content and comfortable, he loved to watch the world go by.

Initially, Bert's bed was set up in the kitchen. During the day, I could go to work, shut the door, and know he was contained, unable to cause havoc. He was still unknown in relative terms. Gradually, he earned the trust, and I would leave the door open for him to wander about downstairs. Occasionally, I would come home to the sofa cushions, dragged off the sofa and all over his bed, providing a little extra comfort to snuggle on his nap. One day I left for work and realised I had left something as I got to the car.

Getting back to the house, all I heard was a scurrying panic. The shuffling and scratching of Bert's claws running down the oak staircase. I genuinely thought he didn't go upstairs as the slippery, spiraling wood was too tricky to navigate. How wrong was I? As soon as the door key turned and he had watched me disappear out of sight, upstairs he went exploring. It was not long before I came home from work, but no dog came to the door to greet me. Worryingly searching the house, I got upstairs to my bedroom to find him, snoring, and dreaming away on top of my pillows and duvet. From that moment on, the whole house, especially the bed, was his, and I would never sleep alone again.

If I did leave Bert alone, it was to head to the cinema. My midweek village life was quiet, and I had a simple rule; if Bert was not welcome, I used that as an excuse to exclude myself. I liked to keep myself to myself. In the village lived two girls who worked at my school, and we occasionally went on a drive into the city to catch a film. One of the girls had a young black Labrador called Millie. It was perfect. The dogs would usually keep each other company in one of our homes for a few hours. Millie's owner found new accommodation in a large but old and cold farmhouse. It was the first time I had ever taken Bert there to leave him with Millie for a few hours. The fear I experienced on my return was colossal. One of the cupboard doors had been forced open, and a rat catcher was empty – the poison gone.

We panicked. We did not know what to do, and we did not know which of the greedy Labradors had eaten the contents. We phoned the local vet and were forwarded to an emergency vet; bring them straight to the veterinary hospital. Being in a rural location, in the middle of nowhere, and neither of us being local, we had no idea where we were going. I remember dark country roads, winding and bending. I remember speed. We arrived at the vet hospital to find a veterinarian outside waiting for us. She asked us which dog swallowed the rat poison, but when we could not confirm, she pulled out a large syringe; both dogs were injected to induce vomiting. All we had to do now was sit and wait. When both dogs' whole bodies began to retch and vomit, it became clear which dog ate the poison and which was unfairly punished. Millie vomiting large quantities of blue, powdery poison, and Bert vomiting only bile. I remember the absolute guilt of watching my boy, my poor boy, spending close to an hour gagging and regurgitating nothing but bile. His stomach was empty, but he could not stop and throughout it all, giving me the pleading puppy dog eyes – why have you done this to me, dad?

Thankfully, Millie was fine and dandy and is still going strong many years later.

## Airdrie

At the weekends was a chance for a change of scene. I worked at a very small rural school on a Friday and finished at lunchtime. We left straight after work and headed back down the road to the family home for the weekend. I still had most of my world down the road – family, friends, social life, and football. Bert loved it. Let the weekend begin.

Bert had a season ticket for my football team. The old 'two men and a dog' accurately described that level of football. My dad and Bert used to always be at the sides. He would perk up when I was near him on the pitch and sometimes try to plod onto the park to say hello. Most of the time, Bert just capitalised on an opportunity to grab a nap on the sidelines. We never had a fear of him going off to chase the ball. When the manager gave our team talk and tactics at halftime, I would always be off scratching and rubbing Bert – much more important.

During this period of my life, I still often frequented the local 'alehouse' for a chat about the game and a catch-up with friends. Bert was perfectly content and happy staying with my parents until I got home. He spent his time staring at Granny Jean's toast with vast quantities of drool oozing onto her legs as he waited. He was treated like royalty. It was never a dinner of biscuits at the weekend; it was chicken thighs, liver, mince – all his dinners were to a very high standard. Bert, and Alfie, were the apple of my parents' eyes.

My father is a typical, old-fashioned Scottish gentleman from a generation taught to suppress or repress emotions and not to wear your heart on your sleeve or express your feelings. On one occasion, my parents were in bed when my mum heard my dad spontaneously whisper, 'I love you'. She was in shock. Those words, which she never doubted but longed to hear. As she rolled over to return her feelings, she noticed he was staring, gazing into the dogs' eyes as he declared his endless love. She never complained. Her feelings were exactly the same, totally besotted.

Anytime Bert visited his Granny Jean's, he was given jobs to pay his way, primarily chief dishwasher and spill response team. This role became more lucrative when Baby Elise was introduced into the family. Bert would place himself directly underneath the front of the highchair, knowing there would be some accidental and non-accidental spillages of food coming in his direction.

They say the only thing a dog cannot do is talk; however, Bert was a fabulous communicator. He communicated through body language and, occasionally, through vocalisations. Bert portrayed emotions through his tail, his ear position and body movements. However, it was his eyes he used most effectively. The Scots have a word 'groak' which means to gaze longingly at someone else's food in the hope they may share with you. Bert loved to groak. The University of Cambridge discovered a genetic mutation in some Labradors, which does not send a message to the brain to let it know the belly is full. This explains why some Labradors are on an endless journey to eat. Although only around a quarter of the dogs had the genetic flaw, the rest are just charlatans. Despite his appetite, he was well-behaved, displaying self-control and discipline. Most of the time. The problem was there was not a member of the family who did not want the gratification of sharing their food with him. We could leave Bert alone with plates of food, knowing they wouldn't be touched, let alone devoured, unless he was instructed to. It was pleasing to know that as soon as he found his safety, he knew and trusted his next meal would be delivered on time, and he no longer needed to steal his dinner.

Bert only vocalized his desires if it was absolutely necessary. There was no room for misinterpretation. Someone was at the door, dinner was late, or he urgently required to visit the 'little boys' room'. His positioning when he barked identified which message he was portraying. And, if somehow his communication efforts failed to be noticed – Bert was a grabber. His jaws would be placed ever so gently on his victim's lower forearm, and he would guide them to what he wanted – the backdoor or, more frequently, towards food. He targeted women. In my family, they were the weak targets. His favourites wore dressing gowns in the morning, giving him the option of clutching the robe's belt and dragging them to the left-over toast crusts. Both his grans had special items of clothing, dressing gowns or scarves, which they would keep for Bert's visits to encourage the game.

On Sunday mornings, there were even more new walks he got to explore with Alfie. Alfie went crazy with enthusiasm when asked if he wanted to go to the 'field' – Bert, not so much. Although they were both, by definition, in the same field, they were often at very different locations within said field. Alfie was far, far ahead, chasing balls and dashing in and out of the water. He ran on to greet friends spotted in the far distance. We often had to backtrack and check on Bert. Constantly sniffing so slowly, out of sight, over the edge of a ridge. He took his time. New smells to ponder over and assess since last week.

As a Physical Education teacher, I use a 'sports day' analogy to describe Bert and Alfie. Alfie is the one decorated in medals at the end of the day; fast, athletic, and determined. Bert is that child who gets a sticker just for participating – 'It's not about winning, it's the taking part which counts.'

Two homes and double the adventures. The car would be lined with a soft bed, duvets, and pillows to ensure he travelled in style, five-star luxury. Bert and I often drove back late on Sunday to do it all again.

THE DEN AND FUN TRAILS

# FIFE COASTAL WALK

KITTYWOOF - BERT AND FRIENDS

# BLUEBELL WOODS

HAPPY BIRTHDAY TO YOU
HAPPY BIRTHDAY TO BERT

"YOU'D GET A PIECE AT ANYBODY'S DOOR"

EVERY BITE YOU TAKE, I'LL BE
WATCHING YOU

JUST A DAD AND HIS BOY

# 3. A Mother's Love

When mum came on the scene, quite worried I would be
Perhaps she'll steal my dad; he'll have less time for me?
But I couldn't be more wrong – instead of getting less
Love for me now doubled as my mum was just the BEST!!!

The moment that I met her, I knew with all my heart
That we would stay together, and this was just the start
Of years of love and cuddles – she filled my life with joy
How proud was I to know that I'd always be HER boy?

I still remember clearly our first walk to Alyth Den
Mum got lost and panicked – that's the moment when
She knew that she could trust me to take her safely back
Life was even better now that mum had joined our pack.

She held my lead so tightly in case I ran away
Or maybe get excited and chase a dog to play
But very soon she realised, that was not for me
I was happy just to plod along by her side you see.

So, mummy stuck around, at her flat we often stayed
On her doorstep was a park where we always walked and 'played'
On return, I'd always pause. Have a seat. Take my time
Living three floors up – that's a lot of stairs to climb.

When we stayed in Glasgow, I loved our weekend morning strolls
Food dropped from the night before – pizza, chips or rolls
The joys of the big city, such treasures I would find
Nose firmly to the ground; no goodies left behind.

Walking through Queen's Park and round the boating pond
With each and every step, we're building up our bond
Then back to all those stairs – I couldn't cope with that
I wished with all my might that she'd bought a ground floor flat.

**Anderson Graham**

That Christmas, I recall, we were staying at mum's flat
Lots of lovely presents were laid out on the mat
Markies, chews and gravy bones – those were smells I knew
They surely won't be missed if I just eat one or two?

But temptation was too much – I ate the bloomin' lot!
Not thinking for a moment that I just might get caught
You woke to empty boxes all scattered on the floor
And funnily enough – my belly was quite sore!

## The Life and Adventures of Bert

I often went on journeys up and down the road
Dad warned he must drive slowly, with his precious load
I never found it challenging, or a stressful chore
When I heard the engine, I'd just lie down and snore.

Mum took a leap of faith, and made a massive move
She sold her flat, quit her job – and boy did I approve
For now we'd be together – three would share the bed
Can't wait for new adventures in the days that lie ahead.

We'd all set off together to climb up Alyth Hill
Or other fun adventures that I remember still
You planned a life together – which of course, included me
And life was even better now that we were three!

**Anderson Graham**

Alyth Hill, a favourite, when I was young and fit
Early to the summit, the bench to rest a bit
Though in my later years, may not make it to the top
Those moments spent together, I would never swap.

# Chapter Three: A Mother's Love

Three's a crowd.

That must have been Bert's initial concern. For several years, it was just him and I; walk, eat, sleep, repeat. And then Dawn came along. The end of an era.

In 2016, Dawn and I started dating. We were heading towards a potential relationship, but of course, she required to be vetted. It is simple – if Bert didn't like someone or someone didn't like Bert, there would be no future. He was my everything.

Our relationship was more miraculous and precious to me than any relationship I had forged with any human – only rivalled by that of my parents (and I'm only saying that because I know they'll read this). Bert shared my good times and vastly improved the bad times. Bert displayed unquestionable loyalty and devoted the best part of himself to me. I had a dog which, at times, I did not deserve, but he had chosen me as his best friend, and I was determined to be a better man worthy of that honour. Bert never sought a perfect superior. For him, I was enough. In this world, of which there are literally billions of people to who I mean nothing, for that one soul, I was his whole world. He worshipped me with endless adoration, which was the most incredible feeling in the world. I would do nothing to jeopardise his happiness.

The worry didn't last for long. To put it simply, it wasn't long before Bert was the love of Dawn's life, and although he already had his soul mate, he was fond of her from the very beginning too.

When Dawn first laid eyes on Bert, she thought, 'what a big beautiful golden boy'. She was also wary as he was a BIG boy. She was chucked into the deep end meeting Bert and my parents at the same time. I opened the door to their home, and Bert came pounding down the corridor towards us. Four paws thundered across the floor in her direction. That initial second of caution as he jumped up towards her was quickly banished as it was clear it was exuberance. Looking down at this dog skipping in front of her, with his big beautiful soulful eyes staring at her, if there ever was a moment she knew the meaning of love at first sight – this was it.

That was it. That quickly. Bert was hers, and she was his. They fell in love. Hard and fast.

We had a meal that night, and Bert targeted the newcomer. It was not long before Dawn succumbed to those pleading, pitiful eyes. Thinking it would only be one small bite. However, from that moment onwards, Bert knew he had her at his mercy and that she was a soft touch. For the years which followed, he would stay close by her side for cuddles, rubs and most importantly, her food. From that first meeting, Dawn would never spend a day without Bert being close by, in her heart, or usually on her clothes. Golden hairs would be a constant in her life henceforth.

When we all went on adventures together as a family, Dawn would take the reins and let him off the lead to sniff and explore. One day I went off to work, leaving Dawn alone at my house with Bert. She decided to take him out to The Den for their first ever walk alone together. Just the two of them. Terrified of the potential of him 'running away', he was kept on the lead the whole time. She knew he wouldn't wander off without her. Bert never went far from our sides, but there was an underlying fear that she could not live with herself if anything happened to her beautiful boy. To be honest, Bert was always content being on the lead and participating in a leisurely-paced stroll.

They headed off early in the morning in the direction of The Den. Dawn was confident that Bert knew the way if she should take a wrong turn. People complimented Bert on that walk and on many other walks. He would sit patiently, tall, and proud, listening to all the words used to describe him. Dawn remembers the pride she felt walking the 'handsome boy' that day. Not merely fond but proud of him.

The first destination was down towards the water. Tail wagging, Bert circled before finding the right spot to plop down gently in the river. Bert liked to keep his head high and proud as he sniffed the air, taking his surroundings in without a care in the world. He gave off an impression he was pleased with his current situation. For Dawn, observing his mesmerising aura, he brought a calmness into her life that she needed. She needed him.

None more so than when she got lost. The walk gradually appeared to go on longer and longer. I was at work; she didn't know anyone in the area to phone for directions, and there was nobody to ask in such an isolated spot. Bert stepped up with his knowledge of his land. She trusted her companion to guide her back home. And so, he did. Spotting a familiar road high up above the basin of the valley, they climbed to safety. Bert was smothered with kisses, lavished with treats, and I was not told about their mishap until much, much later.

We visited Dawn in her Edwardian tenement flat in the leafy Southside of Glasgow. A lovely, spacious apartment. However, there was always an issue. The staircase. That staircase was Bert's Mount Everest.

Dawn lived on the top floor. We had to climb a winding stone staircase decorated with ornate floral tiles, three storeys high, to get there. Each level had two flights of stairs, each flight of stairs consisting of ten stairs. Separating each set was a large landing. I always imagined the architect placed the landing there in the knowledge fatigued dogs would need a rest underneath the stain-glassed windows. Sixty stairs to conquer, just to visit his friend.

He would fret at the bottom of the staircase, mustering up the energy and courage to tackle the ascent. Stop, take a deep breath, and a short burst up to the first landing. This process was repeated. Sometimes he made it up two landings with the momentum gathered. Sometimes only a few stairs at a time. On occasion, there were long recovery periods in between to consider his options and if it was all genuinely worth this amount of effort. Every so often, even a short nap was called for. This has now become a tale of folklore or urban legend, but I do have a memory he once made it all the way to the top without stopping, though I may have imagined that to glorify his achievements.

He enjoyed his walks in the new surroundings. Variety kept life exciting, which was very different from his idyllic strolls in the rural countryside. Traditional, trendy but busy. The flat was close to the city centre, densely populated, with fascinating smells left on each street corner by numerous dogs tussling for the power of the territory. We often walked into the vast ground of Queen's Park. A mixture of manicured lawns and naturalised walks rich in wildlife, two ponds, and an unassuming rose garden tribute to Scotland's Greatest Poets.

That first summer, we explored the park for hours. Every direction, every path within, and the circumference around. I would love to tell you this was for Bert's benefit, purely for his enjoyment. It was not. Dawn had discovered Pokémon Go. The game used location tracking and mapping technology on your phone to create a virtual reality where players catch and train Pokémon in real locations. The idea is to encourage you to travel around the real world and visit Pokéstops to earn Pokéballs to catch Pokémon. She was part of her school's senior management team; considered responsible and mature. And here she was, in her free time, walking around notable locations trying to catch invisible virtual creatures. However, Bert benefited from the new hobby. Miles on the legs, extra exercise is always beneficial for an ageing Labrador who had become slightly portly, as had I.

The key differences we noticed on the walks were the people and the culture of interacting with people. Firstly, I should recognise Glaswegians are known worldwide as friendly, outgoing natives with a strong community spirit. In fact, the city was voted the world's friendliest city by Rough Guides readers in 2014 and 2021. However, there was a contrast between how people greeted each other in the quiet countryside and in the city. When approaching someone in our rural location, I was often greeted with and exchanged a hearty 'hello' or 'Good morning. Beautiful day, isn't it?' It could be that we meet so few people that we welcome the small interaction. Or, more realistically, it is more awkward not to acknowledge each other's presence. Since most of us go out seeking isolation, we are very aware when someone pops up in the distance to ruin our moment of solitude. Be it walker, runner or cyclist, extrovert or introvert, there is always at least a nod as they come towards us. On the odd occasion we pass someone who refuses to make eye contact, I am more inclined to ensure I keep the tradition alive with a friendly, but smug and exaggerated, hello.

However, in the city, people are often too rushed or unnerved by the concept of an encounter with a stranger. Possibly it's just too frequent, too many people to nod and smile towards, that there is no point doing so. Perhaps it is much deeper; a fear of interaction in a world where we interact behind a screen and have become socially inept. I find a twisted pleasure in watching people squirm as they walk towards me. The impending dread, breaking out in a cold sweat as they look at their watch or feet, until they are past and clear of any awkward acknowledgement. I appreciate the nod, a raise of the eyebrows, a smile, and brief friendliness. I always reverted to an elderly lady once telling me she had gone through the whole day without anyone speaking to her. You never know how important a simple greeting could be to the other person.

Another difference I noticed, on dreich[1] days, was the fashion. Bert was an old-school, country boy. Strong and determined, tolerating brutal weather. He would go out in any weather. Rain, hail, or snow, he was out, bare naked and accepting. We tried to introduce him to an added layer for protection once. He showed more energy removing it than he ever demonstrated on any walk. Also, he was Scottish, and we all know Scottish men like a breeze to blow freely. However, in the city, young, trendy hipsters of the world had dressed their dogs in turtleneck sweaters or dresses with tutu skirts.

Now, there are many parts of the world where I know some of you will live where dog clothing is necessary. Dog shoes in the freezing temperatures, extra warmth for small breeds, seniors, or short-coated breeds. Also, there are invaluable vests for some dogs with anxiety. I have even converted to putting jackets on Albert and Bera (you'll meet them later) when the heavy rain is stoating[2] off the ground to save them from getting drookit[3]. Also, it saved me time when drying them afterwards. However, when I see dogs out on their walkies wearing clothes with zero practical purpose, clearly uncomfortable and unable to adopt their normal movement range – it's a no from me. In your home, for your own amusement, just for a moment is fine. We all do it!

There were benefits of being in the busy city over the weekend – including the morning after. With the flat located only a short stroll from the shops and, more importantly, takeaway restaurants, Bert became blatantly aware of the potential to scavenge in the mornings. There were leftovers or disregarded late-night snacks on every street corner. The pubs flooded out with people looking for fast food to soak up the alcohol. A few scraps dropped here and there as they staggered up the road. The challenge was to spot it before Bert did. Despite his placid, gentlemanly nature, Bert could, and would, pull like a freight train towards his desired destination. His collar tightening, dragging, determined to reach his prize. Deep-fried Scottish delicacies: kebabs, pizza, chips, or anything even remotely digestible.

Occasionally, he turned the corner first and got to the food before me. Then I was left with a decision; let him have it or wrestle with him, get my hands into his jaws and remove the object. Option two was only used if it was a large or undesirable reward, as it left me completing the walk with my hand covered in saliva. Bert learned fast. He was smart in these situations and adapted his strategy. On one occasion, he was walking normally along the street on his lead, plodding along by my side, and his whole body was excitedly wagging side to side. His tail and bum shaking with apparent smugness and satisfaction. Stopping and looking at him, I could see his face looked swollen and cheeks wider than a Cheshire cat's grin. Attempting to examine him, he tossed and turned, determined I would not give him a quick check-up. The whole time his jaws were clenched firmly shut. Bert's mouth was pried open. Sitting in pristine condition, untouched on his tongue, I noticed an entire Scotch meat pie. He knew if he chewed it during the walk, it would have been grappled out of his mouth and that patiently taking it home discreetly to eat in secret was his best option. Or he was keeping it to energise himself before those stairs!

Bert would set up camp on the hallway floor in his new environment to rest. It was his tactical position to cover all possibilities. He quickly progressed to the side of Dawn's bed. Chin firmly pressed into the mattress, tail wagging and nose nuzzled into her side whilst she rested. Quickly this transitioned from the side of her bed, to on her bed, to snuggled tightly into her neck or lap, whilst offering an ear to rub to doze off to sleep. Dawn realised Bert only wanted three things in life; to eat, sleep and please others. I hope he knew he mastered the third one just by his presence.

Bert was Dawn's personal therapy dog. Dawn had a job with a lot of responsibility and long hours. After a challenging day, he instinctively knew to sit by her side patiently. She would run her hands through his fur or scratch behind his ear. This was purely for her relaxation rather than his pleasure. Maybe a tiny bit for his own pleasure. Always there to welcome and greet her with a wagging tail, wide eyes, and a grin. All the wrongs of the world were forgotten by the company of a dog. It was that simple. They are that powerful.

I like to think meeting me improved Dawn's life. However, I know that meeting Bert enriched Dawn's whole universe.

When in Glasgow, Bert was introduced to Dawn's family. Together they would visit her parents for cuddles and lovely walks up to the village's castle, but mainly for the many treats his granny gave him. He also met her nephews, all three under the age of five. He was so patient and tolerant. He would follow them about, curious and intrigued. He would welcome their embraces, with their arms wrapped around his neck for cuddles. He would lie on the floor and let them use his body as a pillow as they nodded off together. Bert brought such love and joy to many lives. For those young children, he introduced them to a love of animals and dogs, the perfect introduction to the species.

It was at Dawn's flat where Bert began the chapter of his life as a lap dog. Dawn actually sat on furniture to watch television or eat a snack. This was a new concept to Bert, and he wanted his new friend to join him on the floor. He would gently, then deeply under his breath, growl whilst sitting proud, tall, and regal. Refusing to beg but attracting the wanted attention. Next came the huffs and sighs before one lonely bark as a last resort. Dawn would pat the sofa welcomingly. Bert realised she wasn't coming down on the floor to join him. Having used up all his persuasion tactics, he reluctantly accepted and leapt onto the sofa. Bert proceeded to barge and nudge Dawn into the corner to get himself comfortable. He never looked back from that moment. For the mature years to follow, snuggled and nestled onto a cosy chair, surrounded by cushions and soft throws, became his preferred option. He would nod off to sleep, a luxurious lifestyle and comfort every evening.

Our first Christmas together was spent in Dawn's flat. She wanted it to be special and had the Christmas tree set up in the living room, in the middle of the Edwardian bay windows. It looked so festive. Underneath, a few days before the special day, she had placed precisely gift-wrapped presents for Bert and me. She made a rookie error. That night Bert chose to sleep in the hallway instead of the bed. During the night, he came through crying and whimpering. He was desperate to go outside to the toilet. Bert was six at this point, and it had been many years since he desperately needed to go to the bathroom during the night. Clothes on, down sixty stairs and out into the dark of the night. He plodded down, lethargic and slow, but as soon as the door opened to the city streets, his paws scurried quickly to a good spot. It was like Dumbo had escaped from the circus. These were colossal. As we got back up to the flat, the situation unfolded.

Dawn had wrapped Bert's presents under the tree, but one of them involved food. Two large boxes of Pedigree Markies, the deliciously meaty treat. However, all that was left in the middle of the room were shreds of Christmas paper and some scraps of cardboard. He had sniffed out the goodies and eaten two boxes during the night without either of us hearing the commotion. The guidance on the box instructs a Labrador should have up to 38 Markies a week. I think Bert had that many in only a few minutes. They were all gone.

He was looking for sympathy. Sympathy for his gluttony. Sympathy for gorging and guzzling his Christmas presents early. He got very little for his overindulgence. He had to go up and down those stairs many times those next few days as he gradually deflated.

To dogs, all humans have a unique scent fingerprint to distinguish one person from another. Canine cognition expert Alexandra Horowitz states we are all our scent to our dogs.[4] A dog's scent receptors send messages to its brain, which also deals with emotions. What a dog smells can influence how a dog feels. The sense of smell relates to memory. Memories which incorporate smells are the strongest. Bert greeted us when we entered the door, whether we had been at work for several hours or just popped out into the garage for a few minutes, the same way; with articles of clothing. A welcoming gift. The smellier, the better. They reminded him of happiness and security. When Dawn left to go home after a weekend visit, Bert began to miss his friend. Dawn left clothes for future visits, and Bert would fetch items to snuggle into during the week. There were moments of envy on my behalf when I would come home to him surrounded by her clothes rather than mine. There were also potential moments of embarrassment when I returned home to underwear, gathered, and disposed of at the front door. I could only hope these scent garments were collected moments before my arrival and not early in the day for the dog walker to witness.

Researchers at the University of British Columbia discovered sniffing the scent of a loved one could have a powerfully calming effect and reduce stress hormones.[5] Why should it not be the same for dogs? Midweek phone conversations would conclude with "Bert really really misses you", whilst he wallowed in the scent of his new favourite friend.

The relationship was a whirlwind romance. Within the year, Dawn had given up her prestigious role, which she had spent her career building, to come and live with Bert. And me. With her credentials and talent, she had no difficulty being welcomed into a new school in the area with open arms. She sold her flat, and we agreed I would sell mine.

Dawn's flat in the city of Glasgow flew off the shelves quickly. My beautiful, quaint home took a bit more work, primarily removing the evidence of dog. There was dog hair in every nook and cranny, and every carpet fibre was entwined with dog hair. No matter how often we pulled out the hoover, the carpet washer, or on our hands and knees scrubbing the edges of the skirting board, it just continuously re-emerged. Sometimes flecks turned into fully-fledged blizzards, tumbleweeds of fur rolling across the floor.

Our first home together was sold, and it was time to begin a fresh, new journey. We would start our new adventures together as three.

THAT FIRST WALK TOGETHER

# FASHION ICON

NO ONE WILL EVER LOVE YOU
AS MUCH AS YOUR MOTHER

# FAMILY

WHERE LIFE BEGINS AND LOVE NEVER ENDS

ALL I WANT FOR CHRISTMAS IS YOU

# 4. New Home. New Adventures

You chose the perfect home, where all my needs were met
A bungalow – no stairs, nice garden, and good vet
With lots of gentle walks just roaming round the farm
No busy roads or traffic – to keep me free from harm.

Our new house was amazing. I loved it from the start
Everything you'd chosen was chosen from the heart
Life can't get any better, and I truly do believe
We've found our home for life, and we will never leave!

I went to stay in Airdrie as you organised the 'flit'[1]
And each and every day, I would pick up all your kit
Old trousers, tops and t-shirts, socks, and underwear
Hide them in my bed and pretend that you were there!

I loved my gran and grampa, and I know they loved me too
That's where I'd choose to stay if I didn't live with you
Chicken, steak, and salmon like a Michelin 5 Star
Just waiting for the day they'd feed me caviar!

Soon I had a fan club who'd greet me every day
As I strolled beside the field, the sheep would head my way
Like a little band of 'groupies' – ears pricked, all alert
They'd run towards the fence to say, 'Good morning Bert'.

The cows are very friendly; they'd watch me as I pass
Then trot across the fields, through the meadow grass
Reach across the fences and try to get a kiss
Or even lick my ears – I could get used to this.

Everybody loved me – that came as quite a shock!
The kittens from next door and even sheepdog Jock
Alfie, my young cousin – my uncle's handsome lab
And Buster, a wee rabbit – well, he was pretty fab!

Talking of wee Buster – he was a gentle soul
When it came to mealtimes, he'd race me to the bowl
He'd tuck into my dinner and often make me wait
But funnily enough, we were still the best of mates.

The grannies and the grandpas and little folk as well
All made such a fuss of me, my heart would truly swell!
"You're gorgeous Bert, we love you," some words I heard them say
I'd found my piece of heaven – thank goodness I could stay.

But even dogs like me, can sometimes make mistakes
I didn't always 'plop' in the freshest, cleanest lakes
So happy when I wallowed in a deep hole full of mud
Buried in the earth like a freshly planted spud.

The consequences were worth it, home for my bath
Quick! Protect the carpet, lay towels in my path
Lathered with shampoo, massaged behind the ears
I always frowned in photos, but I loved it all those years!

Life was just idyllic with my brilliant mum and dad
You took me lovely places, and boy was I so glad
That every walk we went was suited to my pace
I'm so glad you remembered – life's a journey, not a race!

Whether it was fields of gold – or fields of fresh sheep poo
It never really mattered, as long as I'm with you
Each walk was very special, a memory being made
Those adventures live forever – in your heart, they never fade.

On a neighbouring estate, there's a lovely little pond
Another special place, of which we were quite fond
No jumping in the deep end – the shallow end is fine
And 'plomping' down to rest, that simply was divine!

And by the River Devon, there's a perfect place to stop
I'd head down to the stream and do my trademark 'plop'
Just lie there, simply chilling, with the water running by
Sniff the country air as I gazed up to the sky.

You'd take me to Loch Leven – we had to go by car
And then when we arrived, I wouldn't go too far
A wee 'plop' in the water, then up, and head for home
But dad, you are the best cos you didn't even moan!

Deep down in the valley, this little gem we found
With rolling hills of heather and beauty all around
'The Devil's Pulpit' waterfall was magical to see
A little piece of heaven for mum and dad and me.

We'd plod along the pathway – keep it safe and slow
Enjoy some relaxations in the shallow pool below
I lay down in the water, the sunshine on my face
The three of us so happy to have found this special place.

Then in my lovely garden, we got a fancy pod
Where you could sit and watch as I would sniff and plod
At nights we'd watch some movies, snuggled as a three
No escaping for a refill, as I slept upon your knee.

Playing in the garden, belly rubs were cool
But if I'm truly honest – I didn't like that pool!
I know that it was summer, and you tried to cool me down
But sitting in that water only made me frown.

Remember how we loved out playing in the snow?
You and me and mum – such happy times, I know
Especially one winter, when the drifts were really deep
Making special memories that we will always keep.

Snow just kept on falling, and it was pretty cool
Lots of roads were closed, so they had to shut the school
Snowdrifts getting deeper – way up past my knees
It's amazing that my vital bits didn't start to freeze!

Trudging through the drifts then hiding in a mound
You gave a little whistle to see if you'd be found
Mum was trying to film us and laughing all the while
Memories of that day will always make you smile.

I never chased a ball unless it's made of snow
I'd skip and jump in joy – hurry up and throw!
A sudden dash of pace, then catch it as it rolled
I'll always chase the snow, even when I'm old.

Now that we were settled, I needed doggy care
And luckily for me, Juliet was there
You told her I was stubborn and certainly don't run
But still, she took me on, and boy, did I have fun.

Fido's Friends were awesome. I had lots of nice, new mates
Who'd 'run' and 'fetch' and 'catch' – the normal doggy traits
I'm sure it must be fun – so please don't get me wrong
But none of that's for me. I prefer to tag along.

# Chapter Four: New Home. New Adventures

We found the most beautiful home in the countryside for Bert to explore and enjoy. It was secluded, hidden from the road by dense forest and vast fields, without being isolated from civilisation.

Dawn and I went to view the house on our own. We fell in love. It was perfect for us. For our situation. For Bert. I always remember my first steps in the house – carpeted underfloor heating. It was delightful; I knew this would help alleviate his aches and pains. By this stage, we knew he was stiff and always tried to stop him from laying on cold kitchen tiles. It was also a bungalow and one of the main reasons we went to view the property. My previous home had a steep, oak staircase; at times, it was like watching Bambi on ice when the now older Bert tried to navigate down the stairs, which always worried me. We loved the bungalow, so we had to come back with Bert. I will never forget that visit. We explored the trails around the property, and it was surrounded by rural beauty – glorious. However, when we discovered a river at the bottom of the farm, that was the moment we knew we had to buy the house.

Bert carefully tiptoed on and over the smooth pebbles, walked in a circular motion and collapsed, plop, right down in the shallow flowing river. His front legs outstretched, his four paws and his cushioned belly were all submerged. For the next few minutes, he didn't move a muscle. He was in a state of total tranquillity. I have always believed he enjoyed the flowing, freezing waters against his increasingly aching joints. The river would become the source of many happy memories. He would sit in the river, a quiet spot beneath the bank, watching the water tenderly flowing and twisting past him. He found solace in nature. He had found his home. A retirement home.

Our last house had served us well, but this was a home built for dreams. Where love resides, new memories are created, and our family begin a new chapter together. Our utopia.

We had to stay in rented accommodation for four weeks between selling our property and moving into the new house. Dogs were not welcome. Bert went on an extended holiday to his grandparents' house. I regret not weighing him before and after his vacation. Every night being fed freshly cooked gourmet meals, the best cuts of meat, treats on demand and milk to wash down every meal. He was treated like royalty. He deserved nothing less. We saw him every weekend, but it was hard to be without our boy. The only silver lining was knowing he was in total comfort. It was a great relief to receive videos and photos of him in a bed full of our clothes, seeking our smell for contentment. He had not forgotten us – though a few more weeks of roast dinners, and I fear he may never have chosen to come home.

During his vacation, Bert spent a lot of time exploring on walks with his friend Alfie, but he also had to share the home with Buster, the rabbit. Buster was flourishing in the latter years of his life. My mum took him into her home to give him a better quality of life, and his character shone. He went from being a well-loved but rather lonely wee soul to gaining free roam of a large home and a whole living room designated as his own private bedroom. He was spoiled with lavish salad dinners, overflowing from the top of the bowl. A mix of fresh kale, mint, and spinach, topped with bright red, ripe cherry tomatoes and his favourite – beetroot. He had become accustomed to being 'top dog' in the household.

So, when Bert arrived and was given his dinner at night, Buster was required to show him who was boss. As Bert's bowl was placed on the ground for his dinner, in front of him as he sat patiently, Buster would charge over, shove his head into his bowl, and start munching away. Bert, approximately 40 kilograms heavier, stood back with a look of concern and bewilderment; what do I do? Why is he eating my dinner? Such a gentle, big, friendly giant, he accepted his fate until someone stepped in to save his meal, and the day.

On his return, we slept on the floor together. No furniture or television, just a mattress and three of us snuggling up. It was beautiful. Gradually, our home became furnished, and Bert had to adjust to a drastic change. "Why are you eating at a dining table, daddy and not on the floor?" He learned to adjust, adapt, and rest his chin on the kitchen bench to watch us eat – this will work just fine.

We moved in during the winter and were almost immediately hit by a snowstorm – the Beast from the East. Schools were closed due to temperatures as low as -15°C and snowfall up to 15cm deep in Perthshire. When it comes to snow, the historical Scottish word hordes have found 421 words for snow, even more than the Inuits.[1] Weather, and the ability to communicate how bad it is, has always been vital to our wee island. In order to survive in Scotland, you must come from a long line of weather-hardened Scottish people, descendants of descendants and all that, millennia of evolution and adaptation to the extreme cold. The weather does not drop as low in temperature as some parts of the world, but it's the constant changing of weather and the fact every weather condition; snow, rain, or sunshine, usually comes with a bitter chilling wind. However, the volatility is part of the charm.

The first morning we attempted to leave the farm by car, we came across a neighbour driving back down the single-track road. She had failed in her attempts to make it out of the farm. She went to move over to the passing place at the side of the road to let me past when she misjudged, and her car disappeared down the ditch. I got out to help and ran down the road to get a shovel and to ask the farmer to help. Along came a tractor to pull her out of her predicament. Whilst pulling and reversing, the tractor's back tyres slipped down the ditch on the other side of the road. At this moment, I knew we were housebound for these few days, just us and Bert.

Those next few days will be forever cherished and engrained in my memories and heart. Some of the favourite days of our lives. We trudged through snow trenches, exploring new roads and paths together as a three. Snow blizzards drifted and whirled as snow billowed into our exposed faces. Each step turned to stomps as we forcefully battled and lifted our feet through the abundant knee-high snow. I would run ahead of Bert and hide behind a deep pocket of snow. I would watch as he navigated and tunnelled through a challenging voyage, marching forward to plough the drifts. When he found me in my snow fort, he plastered himself on top of me. Lustily licking my snow-covered beard with a sense of pride whilst we inadvertently sunk and got buried even deeper in the snowfall.

The excitement a young child experiences waking up to a white winter wonderland is only rivalled by that of a dog. They, too, are filled with a sense of excitement and enchantment. Snow has magical qualities that will produce a skip in the step of even the oldest dogs.

On the farm, we would make snowballs in copious quantities. The only type of ball Bert would ever chase. I think he found the motivation in the fact he could be rewarded by also eating these types of balls – zero-calorie treats. Roll them, then throw them underarm low across the ground. As they rolled, they gathered more and more snow and grew. Then along came Bert and munch, munch, munch. In fact, he loved them so much that we rolled up several extra balls and kept them in the freezer. When the snow was gone, our boy could still get the pleasure of the chase – briefly. Yum.

There was one day in the snow we took a wrong turn. Not to exaggerate, well, maybe a little, but the difficulty factor of this trek rivalled Roald Amundsen and Robert Falcon Scott's deadly race to the South Pole. We climbed a hill and then had a choice, head back down to safety or take this path just over the ridge into the unknown. Obviously, we explored. Finding the safest route under the vast snow and the low-lying fog rolling over the hills became our concern, and priority. Where the ground met the sky became hazed as we looked ahead, almost impossible to navigate. The responsibility of knowing Bert, tired but faithful, would follow me to the end, or top, of the world. Imperceptive of the depth, we took each step with caution and hope. Each foot placement was considered, and he followed my tracks to minimise his workload, which had now become an expedition. We were still ascending the whole time, hopeful that the Law of Gravity is accurate and that what goes up must come down. Apparent the firm crust of snow was incapable of supporting our weight, occasionally dipping waist high, we stubbornly trekked on. At times successfully sourcing the route, the next sinking, each step more pessimistic than optimistic. Bert continued to trust my guidance. It appeared there was no end in sight.

Now, knowing the route, we were never in danger or far from home. Still, it was too long and challenging for Bert in that period of his life. He slept through to the next morning's dawn, and we were never just as curious again but much more sensible in managing our environment on future adventures.

Exploring somewhere new was so much fun. The more we explored, the more we realised it was a dog's dreamland. In one direction, a long, single-track farm road leads us into the quaint village; in the other direction, a large estate with two hundred acres of land, forest, and water to explore. The open fields, framed by vast, dense woodland, made us feel small but also provided a sense of wonder.

In such a remote area, leads were only carried for precaution. We didn't have the concern of traffic, except for the occasional tractor. We only rarely came across other dog walkers, cyclists, or runners. Our only bugbear, a source of annoyance in our place of solace, was the leisurely stroller approaching from behind. We put the lead on Bert out of common courtesy to allow them to pass. They would then decelerate to a pace of barely fast enough to remain ahead of us but just fast enough to leave us with an anxious decision to make. Do we slow down and allow them to get ahead so Bert can get off the lead? Or is this a day when Bert has the speed and stamina to overtake and keep that pace long enough to get a clear distance ahead?

The greatest thing about the farm was that there were so many smells to discover. And being a farm, sometimes those smells to explore turned into tastes to explore. The ancient instincts of hounds were rediscovered every morning as we walked through the farm. Dogs are addicted to foul odours. Dogs have up to three hundred million olfactory receptors in their noses, and the part of their brain which is devoted to analysing smells is vastly superior to ours. Bert could sniff out fresh sheep droppings as soon as his paw stepped out the front door. He never stopped to smell a freshly blossomed rose, but a large, flat cow pat in the middle of a field was compelling, a sensory explosion to his refined nose. Dogs live by smells. Their emotions are smells.

A huge, old oak tree stands on the route home, about two hundred yards from the house. It stands alone, and it's grand. This is Bert's tree. Often, I would call Dawn and say we are nearly home, we are just at 'Bert's tree'. On wet days, or when Bert was stiff or tired, we would say, "we are just walking to Bert's tree and back". It became our local landmark. The first painting we bought for our new home was a commissioned piece of Bert's tree. The expansive fields, overlooked by the hills and a yellow dog walking down the road past the tree. The part which makes me smile was that the dog was lagging, at his own pace, behind the two stick figures in the distance.

Sheep were abundant. We were only ever a few steps from the flock as we stepped out our back gate. For some dog owners, that could be a worrying or stressful experience. Not with Bert. I never once saw him show any interest in another animal. No ancestorial hunting instincts or enthusiasm for a chase. To them, initially, he was a dog, a threat, and they were 'sheepish'. Very quickly, it was as if they knew that's only Bert. The animals of the farm learned the yellow dog was no threat whatsoever and just got on with their business without scurrying away in fear. There were occasions sheep or lambs had squeezed under the fence or escaped out a gate, and Bert plodded by our side without intimidation or a second glance. In fact, there were times the sheep walked up to Bert face to face, almost in a kissing motion, and he would just nonchalantly lay down, taking the attention in his stride. He was the farm's unofficial sheepdog, although he would have been useless at rounding them up. Far too much effort.

That official role was left to Jack, an elderly sheepdog. A black and white collie, usually with dirt decorating his fur after a hard day's graft. He was a timid boy when it came to people. He had no time for that; he had a job to do. Jack had worked his whole life on the farm, gathering the same breed of sheep and listening to the same songbirds each morning. Old age was catching up, and like most, he had begun slowing down. He would plod around the farm buildings during the day, but those old legs could shift when he was called into action. I used to love standing at the back gate, or stopping on the road with Bert, watching Jack at work. He would elegantly glide across the field, following closely behind the quad bike and working his magic. He would move the flock down the hills, through the fields and along the road effortlessly. Jack would leave no stragglers behind. The job came instinctively to him. He was a class act.

Any time Jack or Bert met, it was comedy gold. Both boys were older. Both boys were timid and preferred their own company. Each dog would smell each other's scent all day, every day. Battling to mark their territory across the farm. When they met, I was never sure if it was a courtship mating dance or an old western stand-off. They pranced and danced in circles, like an elegantly choreographed routine. Was Jack trying to impress Bert, displaying his vigour? Or was this a confrontation, coolly encountering each other on a dusty road before a Clint Eastwood-style quick draw? They would never physically get close to each other, just strut around each other. Jack, being the nimblest and light-footed, did most of the movement. Bert cautiously looked around to see where his lover/nemesis was approaching from. Bert's drooping tail lifted and wagged during these encounters. He walked around, sniffed from a safe distance, walked around some more, grew bolder, began to approach, and then ran away.

I almost wanted the day to come that they embraced and became best friends. It never happened, but I like to think there was a mutual friendship and respect between the lads.

Also on the farm were large, inquisitive, beautiful cows. Such strong, powerful creatures displaying a mix of boldness and shyness. They would encroach as the herd, stronger together, staying close to each 'udder'. A slow procession, assessing the threat and, like the sheep, concluding it was safe to become friends. The cows had no 'beef' with Bert. They enjoyed nothing more than trying to lick the big man's face with their huge, slobbery tongues through the fencing. He sat and welcomed the affection, and kisses.

Only a short drive away and we reached 'Bert's Loch'. Known to some locals as Loch Leven, I prefer the title that it became affectionately known by on Twitter. There is a lot of history associated with the loch. Mary Queen of Scots was imprisoned in a castle situated on an island in the middle of the loch. She was forced to abdicate as Queen in favour of her one-year-old son James, who would go on to unite the crowns of Scotland and England. In fact, every British monarch since can trace their blood back to Mary; and it all started at Loch Leven.

So, changing the name in all those history books may make it a step too far. Thirteen miles to march around the whole loch, it is fair to say it was a bit of a stretch for Bert. We would select our favourite sections for a short wander and plop. Some days, we would venture for a few miles, enjoying the new fragrances and the joys a change of scene can bring. And then there were the other days we would drive twenty minutes to the loch, Bert would slowly plod down the beach at the loch's edge. He would flop down contently into the chilly water, allowing the gentle waves to brush against, and under, his submerged body. Before his body could acclimatise, he would get up and stroll back to the car. Short but sweet. He got what he required from the trip and managed to miss all that walking shenanigans and malarkey.

I think there was a reason Bert never spent a long period of time or went past the shallow water's edge in lochs or deep waters.

Scotland's lochs are a distinctive part of its landscape. They shaped the land, and they supply drinking water and hydropower energy. However, they are more commonly known, across the globe, as the home of monsters. Vast, beautiful, and mysterious bodies of deep water, often overshadowed by intimidating hills, are the perfect location for tales. Loch Ness, and Nessie, once had a rival, when in 1934, the *Scottish Sunday Mail* reported a strange monster in Loch Leven.

Are they real, though? Well, the earliest sighting of the aquatic monster was in 565AD when a sea creature reportedly attempted to gulp down a local farmer. Luckily, it was banished back into the water by St Columba, who was visiting Scotland to introduce Christianity. During World War Two, the German High Commander had sufficient confidence in the reality of the monster. They had planned to drop bombs on Loch Ness to destroy Nessie, and thereby damage British morale. Nessie will never be apprehended. According to ancient prophecies, the people of Inverness will suffer a violent demise if she is ever caught, so the locals protect their pet plesiosaur.

Bert would go off on lunchtime adventures with Juliet five days a week. He was gentle, loving, and obedient. But he was also slow and stubborn, which I always worried would be a dog walker's worst nightmare when walking other, more enthusiastic, and playful dogs. Juliet accepted Bert. In fact, Juliet loved Bert. He reminded her of her first dog. Bert had that something special that people related to. He went out in small numbers for a group walk, but his favourite days were when Ghillie was there. A beautiful, handsome, long-haired retriever. After accepting Bert wasn't going to bother chasing him, Ghillie spent the majority of the walk licking Bert's ears spotlessly clean. The vets were always complimentary of his ears – thanks, Ghillie.

At my previous house, Bert never had any interest in going into the garden. It was covered in stone chips and surrounded by neighbouring properties on all sides. The garden became his favourite place to relax and sleep in his new home. With the spring and summer, the garden was a picture of colour. Flower buds erupted and burst to life all around whilst Bert pottered. He loved nothing better than to go outside and lay on the edge of the lush, green grass. Nose high in the air sniffing the countryside aromas or staring into the kitchen, observing to ensure he was not missing any food being served. Due to his wonderful nature, we could leave the French kitchen doors open and let him go out to wander, day or night, knowing he would come back in when he had answered nature's call. We never worried about him digging up hardy geraniums or putting stones in his mouth. Also, we were all perfectly aware he was not quite slim enough to squeeze through the beech hedge and escape, not that I think he would have ever wanted to.

We decided to capitalise on this and invested in a garden room. The pod was built with bifold doors to flow into the garden. We could sit and read, or watch the television, with Bert always in view and within reach. Bert would stretch out on the grass with a giant carrot grasped, like a vice, between his immense front paws. The initial plan for the pod was an office to do work, but the reality of the pod was a weekend cinema room. Bert loved to jump on the corner sofa with us and just nod off – until the cinema snacks came out.

We bought the most wonderful house. Bert made it the perfect home. A home full of loving and happy memories.

"AS THE TWO FRIENDS WANDERED THROUGH THE SNOW ON THEIR WAY HOME, DAD GRINNED TO HIMSELF, THINKING HOW LUCKY HE WAS TO HAVE A BEST FRIEND LIKE BERT".

BERT'S ANIMAL FRIENDS

# LET'S GO ON AN ADVENTURE

# MUD TREATMENT SPA DAYS

BERT'S SUMMER HOUSE

AN EXTRA WAY TO ENJOY HIS GARDEN

THERE'S A RIVER ON THE FARM.
IT WILL FOREVER BE KNOWN AS
'BERT'S RIVER'

# IN BERT'S GARDEN

# 5. An Older Gentleman

It was just around this time, the world came to a stop
'Covid' had arrived, and it caught us on the hop
For me, it was a blessing – a strange thing, you might say
But now my mum and dad were with me EVERY day.

And boy, did we have fun. More memories to keep
Lovely walks, adventures, then back home for a sleep
Sometimes, I'll be honest, if you wanted to do more
I'd close my eyes so tightly and just pretend to snore!!

An elder gentleman likes comfort, sleeping in the middle of the bed
Just knowing you were beside me, stroke me on my head
Snuggly between my family, I sit up and stare
Every night I like to make sure you're both always there.

Also, during lockdown, 'home learning' was the norm
You'd organise some lessons that your pupils could perform
Fitness, skills, gymnastics – you'd demonstrate them all
Sometimes in the garden or even in our hall.

You'd be doing sit-ups, a burpee, or some squat
Then I would saunter over; looking pretty hot!
Park my ample booty on your body or your head
P.E. lesson's over, kids – the 'Bert Show's' on instead.

Your pupils, they all loved it – it really made their day
To see the teacher's lessons so often go astray
With viewing figures soaring and ratings through the roof
It's clear who was the superstar; you need no further proof.

**The Life and Adventures of Bert**

Each day you'd post on Twitter to all our lovely friends
Photos, jokes and videos – all of them you'd send
So many kind replies from fans in lands afar
Each one made us realise how truly blessed we are.

BERT the BEAR was famous, had fans from near and far
From all around the world, they said I was a star!
I don't do fancy tricks, I can only 'plop' and 'plod'
So, if I'm being honest, I was slightly overawed!

From Canada, America, and I kid you not – Peru!
New Zealand, Macedonia, as far as Chile too
Europe, Asia, Africa, Ireland, the UK
#Dogsoftwitter friends watched my antics every day.

Stardom quickly followed (it seemed the way to go)
As I became a mascot for Dog Desk Radio!
Even had my story in their glossy magazine
All that's needed now is a knighthood from the Queen!!

There's never been a day that I didn't strike a pose
Be it plodding in the garden or 'booping' with my nose
Faces looking happy, grumpy, sad or mad
Every one is captured for posterity by dad.

Now daily walks and rituals were captured by your lens
And they were quickly posted to all our Twitter friends
The ones when things went wrong, were often deemed the best
Some very special moments that stood out from the rest.

'Zombie Squad' promoted me and daily I'd patrol
To keep us free from harm would always be my goal
Corporal Bert was enlisted, a famous worldwide squad
Who joined him on his mission with their daily plod.

Whoever would have thought that my mum and dad's 'big lump'
Could end up with more tweets than even Donald Trump!!
The Twitter fans went crazy, but I took it in my stride
Although I must admit, I was swelling up with pride.

Then, when lockdown ended, and the visitors came by
I got so excited I'd make a high-pitched cry!
Do 'zoomies' on the grass with my tail up in the air
And give a great big wiggle with my famous 'derriere'.

It really was amazing, as you know I don't do tricks
I couldn't catch a ball, and I'm not too keen on sticks
Prefer to laze around, chewing carrots on the lawn
But 'Carrot Crunching Bert', a brand-new star was born.

As most of you will know – old age doesn't come alone
I had some aches and pains, but I wasn't one to moan
And when my legs got stiffer, no expense was spared
You got me hydrotherapy which showed how much you cared.

I know I should be modest, but I'd really have to say
Those therapists were swooning when I arrived each day
With my luscious, golden coat and 'Cleopatra' eyes
I'd turn on all the charm – as you might surmise!!

Plodding on the treadmill, I had targets now to meet
It also helped a lot when I got a little treat
I must have looked quite fetching as I broke into a sweat
They chose me as the 'poster boy' for the local vet!

For after hydrotherapy, you bought a drying gown
Although it did work wonders, I always wore a frown
Multi-coloured stripes, like Joseph's famous coat
Everybody loved it but it didn't get my vote.

## Anderson Graham

To reach the golden years is a blessing, I would say
Taking things more slowly and relaxing every day
A good time to remember that life is not a race
You still enjoy each moment – just at a slower pace.

But what if my best days are the ones I've left behind?
I know I'm getting older, and my health has now declined
Reflecting on my life – It didn't start so well
But that is not the part on which I wish to dwell.

The past is now behind me, the future yet to see
And what's the point of worry? What will be will be!
My journey's been amazing – a life so filled with joy
I've cherished every moment since I became your boy.

# Chapter Five: An Older Gentleman

With age came health issues.

Until his final years, Bert never had to go to the vets, except for his routine boosters. When he was eight, I stroked and rubbed his belly one evening. Upside down, four legs flailing around in the air, eyes tightly closed, he was just enjoying the sensation. I noticed his testicles were enlarged and hard. The vet quickly confirmed it to be a tumour. The vet was perfectly relaxed about the situation, confident it would not have spread. With surgery to remove the testicles, Bert would be fine. They were right. But that wait for the phone call to confirm our older, overweight dog was awake from anaesthesia and healthy was torture. Under the knife, they found an unusually large swell on his tonsils which required removal. Two surgeries in one day. Two birds with one stone. Thankfully, both test results came back benign.

However, part of Bert's problems, I believe, stemmed from his recovery. We were told for the first few weeks to only take Bert out to do the toilet. Walk minimal distance and home. When we were allowed to go further, set free to explore the world, Bert was reluctant and seemed happier with his new lazy routine. Dogs notoriously gain weight after being neutered, which can cause changes to the dog's body and incentive to exercise. Despite this, he was still insistent on going on walkies to the toilet. Bert was houseproud and determined to keep his lovely garden tidy and clean. Some mornings he was slowly trootling[1] in the morning sun, and on others, his footsteps were quick to get the job done and back home before getting wet and drenched.

He was a gentleman who wanted to ensure he had privacy as he went about his business. Bert sheepishly reversed into the long grass along the field perimeter. He sniffed, sought, and circled to flatten his chosen destination to avoid an unexpected tickle on his bahookie[2]. His trusting eyes were locked onto me to ensure I was keeping guard whilst he was at his most vulnerable. His walks became gradually shorter, his weight slightly increased, and he got stiffer. Then diagnosed with osteoarthritis.

Arthritis had snuck into his joints; he was weaker, and everything became more laboured and slower. We were told about several options, including physiotherapy and acupuncture. We decided to try hydrotherapy, the best decision we could have made for Bert.

In the first hydrotherapy session, the most daunting part of the experience was that we had to put Bert on the scales. He had put on weight since his surgery, and the long, hard road to shift it was about to begin.

The girls at the vets were besotted by Bert from the very beginning. They took it easy on him during his introductory session. He strolled into the big glass tank, relaxed in all outward appearances. Still, his face expressed concern and alarm when water slowly started entering and increased in depth. This is a dog who only went into water ankle high to plop down, but here he was, in a bright orange life jacket and water right up to his backside. There was no escape. As if that was not bad enough, the treadmill started moving. Gradual and slow but moving. Bert attempted to anchor his bum on the floor, but it did not work. He was forced to get those legs working. Treats were dangled, coaxing him forward. The saliva drooling from his lips only increased the water level. His paws pitter-pattered, scuttling him forward, his mouth eagerly reaching for a bite. Every so often, a lunge would clutch the food out of my unexpected hands, to his immense satisfaction.

Over the weeks, Bert progressed and grew fitter. His stamina and speed on the machine increased. From walking to trotting, then on to a canter. From thirty-second spurts to three-minute bursts. His weight was dropping from session to session. His 'wobbly' gait had vastly improved; he regained a much narrower stance, and movement was more balanced. Things were on the up.

After his session, Bert was served and pampered by his two new lady friends. They would shower him, lather him in shampoo, and blow-dry his velvety golden locks, leaving them soft and sleek. Showers and baths; he never enjoyed them but merely tolerated and stood in acceptance. He then stepped into his magnificent technicolour drying coat. Rich in colours; red, white, blue, and gold. Dressed in his robes, he stood expectantly, waiting to be carried and delivered into his carriage to go home. The idea of jumping up into the car's boot was preposterous as he looked up woefully. We had a ramp to allow him safe access to and from the car. However, it scared the bejesus out of him, and it was retired to the garage, never to be seen again. Bert would scratch and scurry in panic as soon as his paws touched the surface in a desperate effort to escape. He was always fully aware that I would squat down, wrap my arms around and underneath his body and lift him into place. Unwilling to allow him to be undignified. He was gently placed on a memory foam bed, surrounded by pillows, to recover and rest after his workout.

But then the world was hit by COVID-19, and our world would change. Forever. For the better. And the worse.

Hydrotherapy suddenly stopped, and no one knew for how long. This worried us. Would Bert's remarkable progress be lost? The pandemic was initially something no one knew too much about. Would it be days, weeks, or months? Bert could not be seen by a vet without an appointment and without it being an emergency. Any minor concerns with his movement were discussed via video attachments through emails, without anyone closely examining for any underlying issues. When considering these factors in Bert's life, I will always agonise over the 'what if'.

We worked hard on Bert's diet throughout this process. Bert was overweight, but he had always been heavy. Even that first weigh-in, when his ribs were clearly showing. However, he was now a weight which caused him difficulty in physical movements and was putting excess stress on his joints. It was gradual and had crept up over time. A few pounds each year until we got to the stage where it became difficult to rectify. A vicious circle. He was older and needed to lose weight, but he was older and moving less. So, our only solution was diet.

We researched a new diet, and whilst doing so, we discovered Bert was also anaemic after a routine blood test. This gave him a welcomed excuse for his feeling lethargic and shortness of breath. More iron-rich foods made it onto the plate; red meat, oily fish and green, leafy vegetables. Sardines became part of the staple diet. Kale and spinach were steamed, alongside broccoli, to complete the meal. If spinach could make Popeye the Sailor man 'strong to the finish', Bert would give the green stuff a shot. Thankfully, his enthusiasm levels never changed – food was food. The dish was still licked clean.

From the early days, mealtimes were always a well-established ritual. He would be asked if he would like breakfast or dinner. He would reply with an excited skip, whimper, and ferocious tail wagging. The food would be plated and placed in front of him. Bert would appear to sit, but his eyes were pleading and his mouth salivating. The magic words 'good boy' would be followed by a lunge towards the bowl. Every scrap would vanish, and the bowl would be inspected and licked thoroughly to ensure every trace was enjoyed. The same time every day. He knew the script by heart.

The one change – gone was his 'lick' of milk. From day one, Bert got a slither of milk after a meal to wash it all down. It was his luxury treat item. However, cow's milk makes it harder for the body to absorb iron. It seemed cruel so late in the game to change the goalposts, but it was for his own good.

During this uncertain period, with restrictions on our whole way of living, we could not see or spend time with family. As a three, our silver lining was we got to spend almost six months together every day. I will cherish those days forever. Dawn and I were required to work from home and deliver 'Home Schooling'. Bert was never alone.

We had a routine of getting up early and going for a walk as a family through the countryside before going home to set the day's lessons for the pupils. I would often slip out for a short walk again with Bert whilst waiting for their responses. Bert could relax and sleep contently, knowing his mum and dad were with him. Whenever the word 'walkies' was called, Bert began his pandiculation routine to reset the muscles and body for the upcoming movement. He would stretch and push his forepaws forward, lengthening his back, before slowly getting back to his feet with a giant yawn. Bert was ready for his next adventure. He did appear genuinely happy. We grew thankful for where we had the privilege of living during this challenging time, having so many beautiful and secluded walks on our doorstep.

Bert loved to play 'cat-and-mouse'. Not with other dogs but with us in the house. In a confined space where his lack of endurance levels was not exposed. He would suddenly pounce up to indicate the game was beginning. I would be at one side of a table; he would be at another. The object of the game was simple; Bert would chase me and try to catch me, and I would try to keep the barrier between us to prevent him from doing so. It was a game of speed, stamina, and strategy. If he ran clockwise, I would run clockwise. It was a high-level decision-making game. He selected when to use his momentum and keep running in that direction or when to put on the brakes and switch directions to catch me off-guard. He would feint back and forth a few times. Eventually, when I had some distance between us, I would dart for the bedroom and onto the bed. Following, pounding the floor with purpose, Bert would burst into the bedroom and leap onto the bed like a gazelle. He caught me. He won. And then usually had a moment of well-deserved recovery. He never lost that joy of playing or living.

We tried the same game with Albert and Bera with a hugely different outcome. They do not have respect for the game, or the patience to be cognitively challenged. Instead, they just leap on or over the table and complete the game in seconds.

During 'Home Schooling' Bert became a star. Every day I posted a video for my pupils to try to keep them active and engaged. But then there were the Bert days. I was in the middle of recording a task, and the boy would appear – plodding in and interrupting. It was never my intention to feature the scene-stealer in my lessons. He simply did what he always did and followed me around. At first, I would stop the video and reshoot it, but I quickly discovered that this was way better than what I was doing. I had to give the people what they wanted. He became indispensable, and more and more challenges included the superstar. I would perform squats when he would jump up on me, planking when he would lie down underneath me, or pick up my socks and walk off as I demonstrated a throwing challenge into pans. The views, submissions, and responses significantly increased on the days Bert appeared.

It was about this time, on the laptop or the phone all day checking schoolwork, that I decided to explore Twitter. I created an account, submitted my Physical Education videos, and researched other teachers' activities to engage pupils. It was a practical way to network within the profession and observe innovative ideas to incorporate into my teaching. However, one day I came across a photo of an adorable dog. I liked it. I clicked on a hashtag and found lots of dog photos. I stumbled down a rabbit hole and did not want to leave. Why did I not know this world existed? DogsofTwitter was a portal into a new world I wanted to explore. I created a profile for Bert. Initially, due to his ageing and experiencing health issues, I thought it would be a wonderful way to document his life. Also, it was to back up and store his photos and videos. Small interactions, a few follows, someone commented Bert had paws like a bear...

Bert the Bear was created.

He was never called this at home. Before, during, or still. This name was only a nickname adopted on Dog Twitter, and it stuck. People often tell me they only came across Bert later in life, but he was only on social media for seven months. It was a whirlwind. It was amazing.

I had always been wary of posting about my private life on social media and opening myself up to criticism or ridicule. It takes a particular ego to believe people want, or even need, to hear about your opinions or life. The dog community on Twitter was not like that. People loved seeing, sharing, and commenting on dogs from around the globe. They encouraged it. Often it would be the most mundane of actions. In my experience, people just want to see a dog being a dog; eat, sleep, walk. It is a community of people who love their four-legged friends. Some have devoted their lives to dogs, and others are not currently in a situation to have their own dog. Bert took all of this in his stride. Suddenly a camera appeared as he munched his grub, nuddled[3] towards me on a walk, or snored throughout a night of deep sleep. He gained a faithful flock. Each morning they would revel in watching this old dog, blissfully ignorant to his audience, slowly plodding towards or into a camera. It became a signature move.

There was always that fear of people suggesting dogs are being exploited. Bert was extremely willing to participate for the bribe of a treat to sit for a photograph. It took minimal persuasion.

Throughout Covid-19, it appeared to be a welcomed distraction from the chaos of reality. Our canine companions and all our social media dogs became therapy dogs. Helping people to smile or laugh when they needed it most. Dogs, just being dogs, bypassed language barriers and became globally relatable.

Dawn planned to deliver a 'Paddington Bear' topic for school. She thought it would be interesting to see how many countries in the world we could find dog friends to say hello to the class. The plan was to make a fun and engaging project for her pupils. The overall aim; hope we could make it to 'Deepest Darkest Peru', the home of the infamous bear. It was at this moment I realised how far the power and love of Bert stretched. Every continent in the world (except Antarctica – boo you, Antarctica) got in touch with pictures, posters, and comments for the class. We even achieved the Holy Grail; a photograph of Paddington Bear on Machu Picchu in Peru. The kids loved it!

Bert joined and swore his fidelity and allegiance to the Zombie Squad. A group of specialist dogs who are highly trained in the art of stealth and destruction – of zombies! In reality, some dog friends went on walks and posted to claim they were keeping their regions safe and clear of the unwanted. People seemed to enjoy Bert's early-morning patrols. Strolling slowly along the farm road 'in stealth mode', keeping the sheep and cows on the farm protected from imminent zombie invasions. A hero, it could be said. To join, Bert had to renounce all allegiances to zombies under oath, 'solemnly, freely, and without mental reservation'. He made three key pledges.

1. Lay motionless in stealth but occasionally peek open my eyes to look out for zombies in the vicinity.
2. Always keep my ears open to listen out for the enemy – and any food wrappers being opened in the area.
3. Walk very, very slowly so that I am undetectable to zombies.

It was all a bit of fun. But when I had people tell me Bert was the first thing they searched for when they woke up each morning, to start each day with a smile, I realised that these wonderful dogs could do so much good.

Lockdown created a lot of opportunities to explore. The walks on our farm were perfect for us. Beautiful spots within plodding distance, and more importantly, extremely isolated, and tranquil. However, with outdoor walks encouraged during the pandemic, people began to discover our idyllic, peaceful corner of the world and foot traffic increased. So, like the rest of the community, we explored to find variety.

Our village was overshadowed by Seamab hill, not quite to Everest proportion but steep and challenging enough for us. We tried, and we failed. It was just too much excursion for the old man. Panting heavily, shoulders shrugging up and down, and all four feet braced to the floor, his bright brown eyes pleaded with us to stop. Those days were done. (Actually, I think it was Dawn who was struggling the most and used Bert as her excuse to stop.)

We decided to hike a smaller hill range on the other side of Seamab. They were steady, gradual, and more manageable. The views were even better; panoramic. They sat above three reservoirs and were surrounded by mountain ranges as far as the eye could see. This became our weekend exploration spot. All week walking underneath their shadows, they were the giants on our horizon, every day surrounding us. At the weekend, they called us. They beckoned us.

Off we set over the hills and far away, searching for our special day. We would amble and have several stops along the way. Bert took his time, head close to the ground, and sniffed the whole history of the path. That same path which had been explored and travelled by generations of dogs and walkers. A challenging path but a rewarding one. We would sit together, side by side, and just take in this picturesque part of the world, with its vast untameable hills and deep daunting lochs. Surveying his kingdom. A beautiful spot that we were lucky enough to call home.

After conquering our challenge, we had a proud feeling at the summit. The green rolling, rugged landscape; a land engulfed in history, tradition, and pride. We were immersed in magic and mythology, the sense of being transported to another world. We were reminded there is nothing small about our wee Scotland. I loved those moments. It is remarkable how much a dog can allow you to see. We would sit down, side by side, and take it all in. It would be early in the morning, and we would be the only ones on the hill. It was our moment of solace. Tranquillity. Unavoidable nothingness, broken by only ragged breaths and percussive heartbeats.

Word of mouth brought us to The Devil's Pulpit. It was a short drive out of town with extremely limited parking, so we arrived before the break of dawn. A brief hike through some woodlands and a small meandering river took us to a dusty, terracotta red path which looked like it belonged at the base of the Grand Canyon. Bert glowed as the sun began to appear from over the hills ahead. Shining through the valley and enhancing the colours all around. His coat golden, the sunburn orange sun reflecting off the path; Bert beamed. He was perfect that day. The walk was longer than we expected. Several stops, plods, pauses, and then we saw it. We were walking alongside a narrow stream, through the green valley, and a charming waterfall appeared ahead of us. Water flowed down the cliff front, drizzling down the rocks and into a plunge pool below. The water was varnish clear. Bert's legs accelerated along the meandering path until his whole body was submerged in the pool. That boy did not move for several minutes, with the waterfall's flow brushing against and around his sides. I could not stop staring and admiring him. It appeared silent despite the murmuring winds, chirring grasshoppers, and the water splashing from great heights. He was tired. He was probably sore. But at that moment, watching him in a place of total pleasure meant everything to me.

A few weeks later, we returned one more time to bring mummy with us. Knowing the distance, we managed the walk better this time. Scheduled, prolonged breaks in watering holes were introduced. It was worth it for some of the best photographs of Bert, which I will cherish until my final days – I hope Bert found it worthwhile too.

That summer, Scotland had a heatwave like a tropical island. Many of you would snigger and laugh if I told you the temperatures. Possibly even shiver in your warm woolly sweaters, but it is all relative. We are a cold, wet nation. Any sun is a cherished gift or can be our worst enemy. For some, anything above our typically low temperatures, to which our peely-wally skin has acclimatised, forces us to either complain, melt, or hide in the shadows. However, it is an unwritten rule for others to get their 'taps aff' [4] when even the slightest hint of sun peaks through the clouds. In Glasgow, when the taps aff point has been reached, usually about 20 degrees Celsius, it is universally deemed appropriate for men of all ages and sizes to remove their tops. In other tropical spots across the world, the removal of clothes is confined to the beach, but in Scotland, when the sun's out, you'll find topless men anywhere and everywhere.

With Scottish summers and temperature increases comes the compromise – the midges. Most visitors gloat about experiencing our country's beauty, but many also experience the misery of meeting the 'Highland midge'. The almost silent hum coming from a swarming cloud of dots which gather near water is the sound of teeny-tiny vampires looking for a feast. From dusk till dawn, minuscule in size but grand in annoyance, they irritate every man, woman and child who dare cross their path. Eight thousandth of a gram in stature but hunting in packs like wolves, entomologists claim they do not bite, but I am sure this is to save our tourism trade. If you ever see a Scotsman swiping, swinging aggressively in vain at the sky and their own face, hurling expletives; they are under attack, and you should run away. It made visiting Bert's favourite watering holes a chore in the height of the summer, but we sacrificed our well-being to take him to his happy place.

We spent most of our time on walks or recovering from walks. Bert loved to rest in the garden, doing the absolute minimum. This was not always practical. Whenever I wished to cut the grass, I would have to detour around him. I don't know if he trusted me not to chop off his tail with the lawnmower or if he was demonstrating a pertinacious resistance and refusing to move – Go around me. It turned into a game of Chicken – make yourself immovable; your flexibility is a weakness. However, as soon as I admitted defeat and started cutting another section of the garden, Bert would get up and reposition himself on a new, lush, green patch of uncut grass. Right in my path. Repeat. He loved and wanted to always be nearby. I loved that about Bert.

Making the most of the weather, we frequently went out for light sun worshipping sessions, with factor 100 sunscreen smeared all over our bodies. Deckchairs, sofa cushions and pillows sprawled out over the grass or the decking of the pod. Before doing so, out from the garage came any and every large cardboard box we could find. Firstly, we had to build a cardboard castle fort. It was not just because I am incredibly childish, although it was fun. I did want to dig out a moat – I wasn't allowed. We were making a shaded area for Bert to lay near us but hidden from the sun's rays. On most days, Edinburgh Castle is Scotland's largest castle, but I'm sure on these days, Bert's castle rivalled it. It was enormous. He was a big lad who overheated quickly and could pant very loudly when he was hot. It was essential to cool him down, and we tried lots of tricks. He was frequently, subtly, covered by the garden hose on mist mode until he realised that he was most certainly being purposely targeted. At this point, he would rise and try to avoid it at all costs. Other times we drowned the grass around him and let it seep underneath his body as he slumbered. We also tried soaking his robe in advance and draping it over him so he could go outside. It kept his body temperature low without the risk of suffering heatstroke. This method seemed to work; he would lay sleeping, allowing us to gently spray the hose over the jacket, replenish and remain cool. I think this reminded him of the soothing stream.

Cold treats were also introduced, and this is where we discovered the frozen banana. They were mashed up and placed inside a Kong. We were assured the dog would lick away for lengthy periods until every last bit was gone. Nope. Not Bert. For a Labrador who adored his food, Kongs were not for him. He lacked determination and perseverance. He had lived a life of being waited on hand and foot, and this was not about to change. He wanted his food quick and edible. He was not about to work for his food.

Since Bert was used to hydrotherapy, we figured the best solution was to buy him his own paddling pool. It took a LONG time to fill up that pool. Though not quite as long as it took me to blow it up with my tired lungs. Every huff and puff thinking *this is for Bert*. Eventually, we had a lovely inflatable pool, in the middle of the garden, in the beautiful sunshine, just for Bert. Words cannot describe how much he HATED it. He had no interest or intentions of going in that thing. After several failed attempts to coax him in, he allowed me to lift him and then sit in the pool beside him. He stood for as long as he could, only his paws wet, before eventually, reluctantly, sitting down. It was cold. We both just sat motionless, staring at each other. I wanted to get out. He wanted to get out. We wanted to get out. We HATED that pool. The pool mysteriously burst shortly afterwards, never to be seen again!

When travel conditions were relaxed, we spent a lot of our free time trying to take Bert to new beauty spots for new adventures. We set off first thing in the morning to explore several beaches along the East coast of Scotland.

Firstly, Kinghorn was a small but delightful stretch of sand offering spectacular views across the Firth of Forth to Edinburgh. He weaved down the cliffside steps, tail wagging in anticipation, onto the empty beach below. Bert's gentle panting was overshadowed by the loud morning calls of the seagulls overhead in the clear blue skies. Cautiously aware that sand underfoot can exacerbate an unstable gait and may be particularly difficult to navigate, especially if your dog is trying to protect certain painful joints as they move, we always went at his pace. Some dogs will set foot on a beach, and off they go. Digging in the sand, splashing against and into waves, waiting for their ball or frisbee to be thrown to allow them to ferociously stride into the vastness ahead. For Bert, it was all about the new adventures and beautiful surroundings. Bert followed our footprints in the sand towards the disappearing tide. He would sit, sniff, and look around in a moment of solace. Water dripped off his belly onto the shimmering beach. A trot slowly through the firm, wet sand towards the sea quickly changed to a canter in the opposite direction, back to safety, when he saw the waves race towards him. He only did slow running streams, not these large waves crashing down upon him. I never said it, but subconsciously I think I knew I was running out of time with my best friend and these journeys were more of a pilgrimage; for me. We had been restricted for months, and with him growing older, we were wary of always putting off trips till overmorrow[5]. I hope he enjoyed it as much as we did. I loved observing him. Dogs are happy with any walk. They may have a favourite but generally accept what we offer them on any given day. They do not worry about what they are missing. They simply enjoy the moment. If we get caught worrying about the future, the joy and beauty of life will be lost.

Then there was Tentsmuir, where we walked past grassy dunes onto the expansive sands. The sea appeared to remain in the distance, the low tide running away from us faster than we could plod towards it. When we finally arrived, Bert tiptoed carefully on the edge of where the ocean met the golden grains, like he was a tightrope walker in the circus. He made sure not to get his feet wet before exhaustion took over. He slumped into the sea. I joined him to film the sun glimmering, bright, sparkling light onto the handsome boy. Suddenly, caught by surprise, a large wave came crashing from behind and soaked me. The force of the tide's ebb and flow knocked me off balance. Bert saw it coming from his position and moved quicker in that instance than he had in years. Springing to his feet and rushing out of harm's way, every man and dog for themselves. He forgot all the years of devotion and loyalty, disrespecting the motto 'leave no man behind'. I spent the rest of the day with a soggy bottom for the long drive home.

Finally, we ventured back to Elie and the Fife Coastal Path, the favourite from our youth. Too old, too stiff, and too sore. Unable to walk from village to village, we popped out for a stroll before going back into the car and onto the next destination. It felt special this time. We sat on an empty beach together and watched the waves. We wandered to the edge of the lighthouse and harbour before eventually settling down for a rest. Mum lay down on the pier's edge beside her boy. Bert snuggled in even closer. We did not go any further that day. We just sat there, the cold sea breeze soothing against his body, and let him sleep.

He had become content with snoozing for long periods of the day. On walks, he tired long before I did. He would look up at me, imploring me with his beautiful brown eyes. I noticed how much grey and white had crept into his face. To me, there is no more perfect view than an older dog who has earned each grey hair on its muzzle and eyebrows through a lifetime of devotion and service. The senior citizen would sit, anchor himself to the path and, only when he was rested and ready, would we turn around and head back home

Going back to full-time teaching, physically in the school, was a shock to everyone's system. For almost six months, Bert had mum and dad with him, every day, all day. I never had any anxiety about us leaving him. Nonetheless, it had been such a long time since he experienced it, and he had grown accustomed to our ever-presence. He knew his routine, which had not changed for years. He would come to the door, give us our much demanded and required kisses, and receive a carrot in his mouth (or dental stick in earlier years). He would rush back to his bed and munch it away in comfort. The welcome we received when we returned home was precious, particularly on that first day. Bert tip-tapped and skipped in the doorway when he heard to car pull into the driveway. His whole body was shoogling and waggling with excitement for the front door to open. He whined in excitement with a mouthful of clothes, frantically scuttling forwards to embrace us. I think he had collected half of the clothes from our wardrobes to snuggle in and greet us that day. It was my favourite part of each day and the cure for any negativity. Pure unadulterated happiness. I never arrived home to that welcome without a smile on my face.

The house became littered with dog beds. He would have a soft spot to rest by our side where we would settle. He always wanted to be close at this stage of his life. His favourite spot in the evenings was on the large corner sofa, squeezed into his mum. Head smashed right into her lap, demanding his ears rubbed until he had nodded off to sleep.

He quietly groaned in discomfort and effort when he gingerly laid down. He then quietly groaned in discomfort, and effort, when he gingerly struggled back up to his feet. No matter how exhausted or stiff he felt, if we left his side, he wrestled with determination to follow. Right on our heels, plodding heavily behind. Possibly optimistically hoping our destination was the kitchen. Bert could be in a deep sleep, counting the sheep on the farm, heavily snoring and curled up cosily. We would tiptoe silently, sneaking out of the room not to disturb the sleeping giant. And just when we thought we had succeeded, we would faintly hear the torturous regime. Lumbering with difficulty to his feet, dragging himself and clomping to follow us. Too loyal for his own good. Once he was in his new destination, with minimal grace or finesse, he collapsed into position with a thump.

With age also came flatulence. Deep in sleep, Bert's muscles fully relaxed. He could startle himself awake either by the force of the vibrations or when the stench hit his nostrils. He would then open his eyes and proceed to search for the culprit, giving us a look of disapproval for committing such a heinous crime. After shaking his head in disgust, he would readjust his body and fall back to sleep.

For most of his adult life, he wished to sleep on his bed, placed on the floor directly beside ours. I spent most of my adult life sleeping on the very edge of a mattress, dangling my hand over the side to feel him, pat his head or stroke his hair throughout the night. I think he liked to know I was near, and I could feel his stare and know when he needed that reassuring touch. He also brought out that stare in the mornings, urging me to awaken. Waiting for his breakfast time. That was his favourite word. His chin propped up, resting on the mattress, and his excitement could not be contained when he saw my eyes open. His whole body jiggled, knowing he was about to get his prize. Dinner was almost 12 hours ago. By now, he was fading away.

Towards the end, he wanted to spend more time sleeping with us on the bed. He became happiest when wedged tightly in between us both. Tail pounding the mattress in the pleasure of scratches and rubs. When it had worked its magic, Bert's head rested on my chest or across our bodies, and his tired eyes began to close. I would often tenderly place my head against his wrinkly neck. I wanted to listen to my favourite noise and get a whiff of my favourite smell in the world; his snoring and his breath. If either of us dared to leave the bedroom for any reason, we knew on our return Bert would have claimed the best spot to himself. Understanding the unspoken rule that you cannot move a comfortable sleeping dog, we would squirm into the bed beside him with whatever space was available. To be honest, we happily obliged.

Throughout the night, Bert would stretch, brace and push against my back, grunting and shoving for every inch to get in the best position. One large paw was placed on my body, always in constant contact: a chain link that was never to be broken. His body was tired and weary. I think he knew he wouldn't have too many more chances to be by our side and wished to spend every moment pressed against, and beside, the people he loved.

YOU'LL FORGET THE SUN IN HIS JEALOUS SKY
AS WE WALK IN FIELDS OF GOLD

SURROUNDED BY SO MUCH BEAUTY
BUT ALL I SEE IS YOU

MY RAINBOW CALLS ME THROUGH THE MISTY BREEZE OF MY WATERFALL

OH I DO LOVE TO BE BESIDE THE SEASIDE

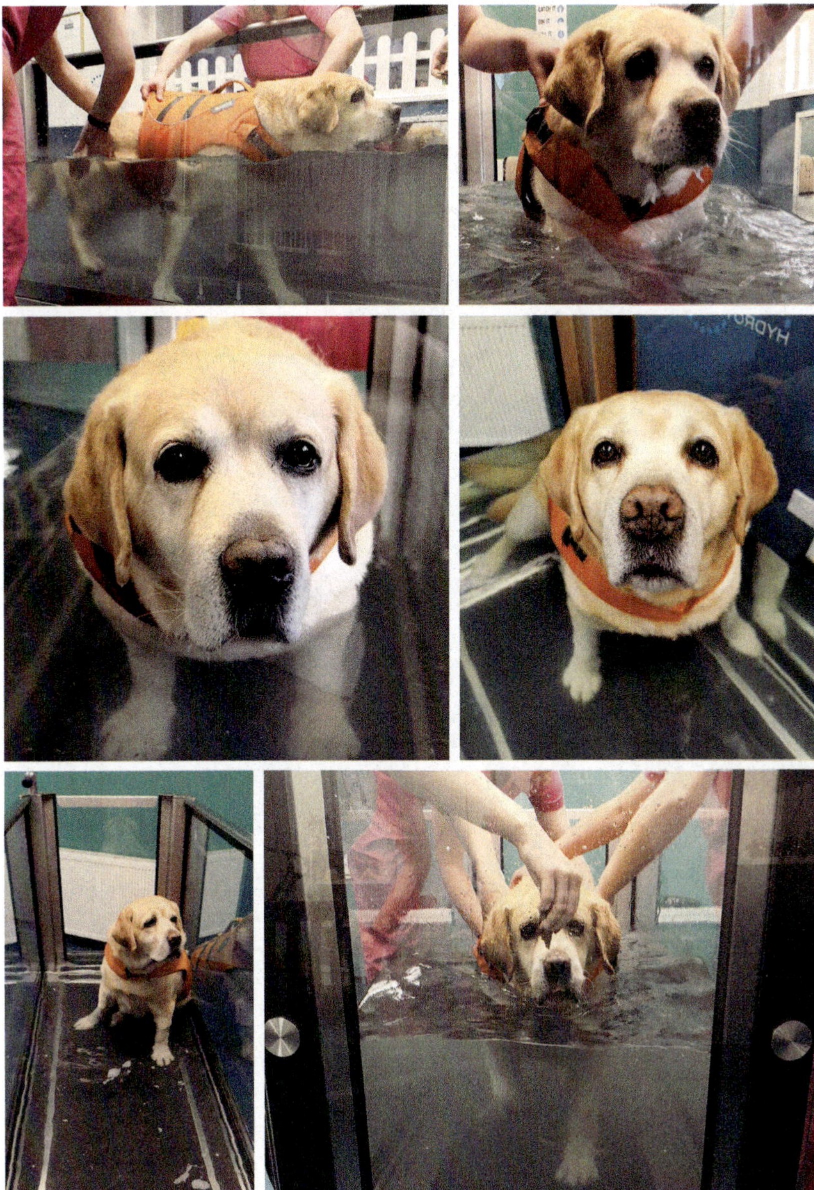

HYDROTHERAPY
"UNTIL YOU DANGLE A TREAT, I AM NOT MOVING"

BERT'S COAT OF MANY COLOURS

DARE TO DREAM - AND SNORE WHILST YOU'RE AT IT

# 6. Goodbye For Now

Then came that fateful day, as summer turned to fall
Trying to get up – but my legs won't work at all
You carried me around like a baby in your arms
Did everything you could to keep me free from harm.

I see the pain and anguish as I gaze into your eyes
You tell me that you love me and our love will never die
You've always put me first and done what's best for me
So now you must be strong. Be brave and set me free.

So please do not feel guilty because we had to part
I knew that I was loved, and it would break your hearts
You saw I was in pain, and I could no longer fight
It was my time to go and what you did was right.

Beside my mum and dad was the perfect place to be
Cuddled, loved, and cherished – to the very end, you see
Listening to you singing our very special song
I'll ALWAYS be your sunshine – forever's not too long.

As I travelled to The Bridge, I felt the warmest glow
No more aching limbs, no more walking slow
'Welcome into Heaven Bert' but this isn't something new
I'd already been in heaven in those years I spent with you.

# Chapter Six: Goodbye for Now

The worst day of my life.

Bert was overweight. However, he was never slim. Even when I found him and his ribs were visible, he had a deep-lying base, a big, wiggling bum and weighed almost 40kg. He was not diagnosed with osteoarthritis until his later years, though I fear he might have lived with the painful condition for most of his life. He was always slow. Always plodded. But he was always happy. He was a warrior. Despite being in pain, he kept living and choosing to love.

It was an ordinary Thursday morning.

I got up, gave Bert his breakfast, and we went for our short saunter along the farm road. It was dark with a light mist, and the sun was beginning to rise behind the hills. I took a video of Bert walking toward me with his trademark slow plod. There was nothing remarkable about the whole incident. In fact, to all intents and purposes, it was a totally unremarkable moment. In the course of a lifetime, you will experience many such moments; mundane, until they are gone. Only then do we realise it was a moment to be cherished. That moment was, instead, a perfect picture of a life which was a miracle. It will forever be etched in my memory.

Bert got a carrot and lay in his big comfy bed, and we left for work. It wasn't until the school day had finished that I noticed I had received a text message from the dog walker, Juliet. It said Bert would not put weight on one of his paws. We rushed home to check, and as always, once he heard the car approach, he laboured to greet us at the front door. Bert was lackadaisical, with little energy except to indulge in self-pity for good measure. We phoned the vets, but it was still appointments only. They suggested we pick up some antibiotics the next day and closely monitor his progress. He occasionally suffered sore legs. He was on pain medication daily. It happens. I am ashamed to say, I was not overly concerned. I was worried about an overreaction from an overprotective owner. He frequently got fresh ice packs placed on his leg to reduce the pain and inflammation in the injured area. He went out, with effort, to use the toilet. His mum and I observed every step, every movement. He hobbled with perseverance, which was to be admired, before squatting with difficulty. He did not always have the balance to cock a leg on four legs, let alone three. Bert then limped back to his bed to relax. We moved his two massive memory foam beds together so he could settle in total comfort. Decorated in pillows and duvets; cosy. Dawn and I set up camp and took turns sleeping beside him in the living room, close to the garden, for easy access. We took progression videos and sent reports to the vets. We agreed that if there was no improvement, we would make an appointment on Monday.

I remember returning from work on Friday, and Bert remained in bed. This was the first time in our eight years that he didn't come to greet me as I was coming in the door. I looked at him, into his big soppy, puppy dog eyes. Physically he had no power, and mentally he looked drained. "You lazy bum. Have you not moved all day?" – I'll regret that joke till my final breath. His tail still wagged with fury, his eyes lit up in great delight that we were home to be with him, but he remained nuzzled low, hopeful, but helpless.

Sunday morning, I woke up on the sofa beside him. Leaning over and scratching his head, we did not make much effort to move. A lazy morning. I patted his head and stood up to take him to the toilet. He would not stand up. I shouted for Dawn, who was instantly hysterical with worry. I supported him onto his feet, but he wouldn't, or couldn't, put weight on any of his legs. I scooped up all 42kg of him like he was my little baby. To help him complete his necessary business, I straddled him, my hands clasped beneath his torso and lifted him onto the grass in the garden. The whole time, I had to hold him up on all fours to keep him balanced, or he collapsed to the ground. My heart sank. Dawn and I were in a panic!

She was insistent we phone the emergency veterinarian straight away. I remember giving Bert a carrot as he lay in the garden and watching him munch it, crunch it – with tears rolling down our faces whilst we made the call. I noticed how much his muzzle had faded, his eyes were cloudier, and his nose had lost some of its pigment; now lighter in colour and beginning to crack. He lay there on the grass and displayed a weariness I had never seen in him before. Despite his 'flaws', he had never looked more beautiful. More perfect. My eyes had always found him the most beautiful, but it was my soul which fell in love with him.

We arrived at the vet, and no one seemed overly concerned. We told them the issue, and they had a look at him in the boot of the car. They (plural, obviously) carried him inside. In the haste of the moment, it was not until he was inside that we realised we couldn't go inside with him. We didn't know what was happening. I remember naively asking, "Will we wait, or will we come back later to pick him up?" We were confused and unaware of what was happening and how long the check-up would take, but we were convinced he was in the best place possible to help him recover.

We called that afternoon to ask when we could come and collect him. We were told the vets would like to keep him overnight to do some tests and x-rays, and they may have to sedate him if he could not settle to take the x-rays. Always a worry for a larger, older dog. That was the first time I was anxious.

Bert had never spent a night since that serendipitous evening when we first met, without having me, Dawn or one of my family by his side. He had never spent a night, or any prolonged period, in a cage or confined space. In his moment of need, I feared he thought he had been discarded once again.

They called me at work on Monday morning, suggesting we had decisions to make. He wasn't better. He wasn't reacting as positively as they had hoped to the drugs. I said there was no decision to be made. He would have his x-ray to discover his underlying issue, they would keep trying the drugs, and we would call later to hear about his progress. That was the most challenging day of work I have ever had the misfortune of experiencing. My mind was only on one thing, yet I still had pupils in front of me to teach. We called back in the afternoon, but no one was available to talk to us due to other emergencies. They would call us back in the evening with an update. We knew we were on borrowed time.

Monday evening, with every passing second growing increasingly concerned, we eventually received a call. It was a much more positive conversation, a moment of fresh hope. They had managed to get all his x-rays whilst he slept. He seemed a bit more alert, even though he still was not putting weight on his legs.

"Great, can we come and see him? Can we take him home? Can we drop off clothes for him to sleep with so that he has the comfort of us?"

"No, sorry. Covid restrictions. However, we will see how he is in the morning, and we can reassess then."

We smiled that night. We hugged and spoke about our future together. That was the first evening we managed to get a good night's sleep. The respair[1], the fresh hope, was a massive weight off our shoulders.

Tuesday morning. Eight-thirty in the morning. We were organising our classrooms to start the day, and my phone rang. It was the worst possible news. Bert was not responding to the steroids. He wasn't alert. He wasn't comfortable. "We think you need to come straight away to see him and make a decision." The night before, they would not let us come over, but a few hours later, they insisted we come as soon as possible. I feared the absolute worst. I ran through the school to Dawn. "We need to go now." Luckily, we had a dog-loving deputy headteacher who, without a moment's hesitation, said, "Off you go." We had trouble processing it all. We knew we were on our way to decide if Bert should live or die. For the first time, there was the realisation of no promise of tomorrow. He had reached an age where death no longer had the quality of being a ghastly surprise[2]. We were always aware that a decision about his mortality would come one day. But not yet. Not today. We drove to the hospital, the whole way saying, promising, we will do ANYTHING and EVERYTHING we can for him. Every drug. Every operation. Refer him to any specialist required. No matter the cost. Anything. Everything.

We rationalised: of course, he is not comfortable. Bert has lived a life of luxury. He is accustomed to sleeping in a super-king-size memory foam bed and is currently stuck in a tiny crate on a drip. He has never been away from one of us. That is all it is.

We got to the hospital and were told to go into the garden, and they would bring him out. I could not wait to see him. Dawn was desperate to see him. Knowing that as soon as he sees us, he will come alive.

Nothing is more devastating than too much love.

My heart has never sunk as quickly as it did at that moment.

My heart shattered into a million pieces. Three veterinarian nurses lifted him out of the building onto a small brown and white blanket they had placed on the grass. He was not alert. He had no excitement to see us. My mind convinced me it would just be the steroids; however, we were assured none of the steroids he was on would cause such drowsiness.

We hugged him. Kissed him. Stroked him. Tickled him. Not one single wag of the tail.

We offered him a treat. No thanks.

I BEGGED him to kiss me, look at me, wag his tail once. Nothing.

He did not have enough strength left or ambition. Bert's face was settled in an expression of desolation and melancholy. He heaved a sigh and dropped his head resignedly upon his front paw.

The veterinarian, witnessing the agony in our faces, told us her prognosis, the options, and the complications. They wouldn't know for sure until the test results came back. We were told all the options. They could tackle the suspected issue with strong doses of steroids, but that would not eradicate the problem. It would only help ease the pain. Recovery was never promised, or even a positive prognosis. At the very best, it would be a long and difficult journey with an old dog, tired and pumped full of drugs, before the postponed inevitable.

I always thought it was just an old wives' tale. An overused cliché. 'They will let you know when it's time.' That day, my boy, let me know. Bert didn't want to be here anymore. It was written all over his face. For eight years, my boy smiled and radiated love. He waggled his tail vigorously anytime I spoke to him or approached him. And that one single day, he did nothing. He didn't want to kiss me. He didn't want to look at me. He didn't want to be there. At all. A dog's ability to communicate is powerful. Bert did not require to be able to talk to tell me what he wanted; what he needed from me that day. What I already knew.

It crushed my whole heart, but when you take on the life and joy of a dog, it is your responsibility to take on the death too. I believe he did not want to look us in the eyes because he knew how much we loved him, and he could not bear to witness us in so much pain.

Dawn, holding onto her baby boy, and my parents, on the phone, both crying, all pleading we need to do anything and everything. He is going nowhere!

I do not know where I found the bravery to say no. To have the absolute clarity of heart and mind to understand that Bert's quality of life was over; a decision unclouded by sentiment. This is not the Bert I know. This isn't fair. He's miserable, and as much as I always joked that he was a miserable old man, that boy just oozed love and joy when he was with his family. Bert pleaded with me that day to please let him go. I listened. And it destroyed me. It wouldn't have been Bert's idea of a good life. It wouldn't really have been a dog's life.

Bert showered me with too much love for me to ever allow him to suffer or to be in pain for a moment longer. I made the decision to let him go, physically, from my world. Knowing I was making my world a much darker place and that life would never be as good, as perfect, ever again. I was brave. I was selfless. And I hated it.

There was a poem I heard as a child which had stayed with me. I resonated with 'Do not go gentle into that good night' by Dylan Thomas. I always focused on that line, firmly believing that we should fight fiercely and bravely against death. On that day, it was another line which had a new perspective for me; 'though wise men at their end know dark is right'. Bert knew his body was failing. He had battled on as much as he could. Bert didn't want to fight anymore. He was not scared to die. He wanted to escape, and my responsibility was to allow him a dignified, peaceful submission to the inevitable.

The vet told us to take all the time we needed and left us alone to lie in the sun with our baby. We cradled him, kissed him, and let him hear every thank you he ever deserved for loving us. For making us happy. For making every single element of our lives better just by knowing him. Eventually, the vet came out with the euthanasia shot. She talked us through the process. I held my boy, as tight as I could, breathing heavily with panic and my own pain, and sang:

"You are my sunshine, my only sunshine
You make me happy when skies are grey
You'll never know, Bert; how much I love you
Please don't take my Bertie away."

He was sleeping, snuggled deeply into and against his loving mum's chest, whilst I cradled his head. He began to snore. He was the most comfortable and relaxed he had been the entire day. We received his final moments of love. He was at peace and comforted beside the ones he loved the most. I like to think it is how he, or any dog, would have dreamed of leaving this world.

The drugs for euthanasia were gently fed into his bloodstream. He passed much quicker than I could ever have imagined. He gave a silent ghost of a whimper. It sounded like relief. Bert put up no struggle, no fight, no panic, no pain. He put total trust in us. The vet listened to his heart and told us that he was gone. My best friend, my baby boy, no longer would be with me, by my side, every day, wherever I go.

On the 29th of September 2020, Bert's mission to fill the world full of love and compassion was complete. The time was 11.11am. Angel numbers – fitting for the guardian angel who saved my life. People often tell me how I saved Bert that night, but the truth will always be that he saved me. He gave me a purpose. He gave me responsibilities. He let me experience what it felt like to love someone more than you love yourself.

I scooped my boy up and we took him home. We placed him in his bed, and we spoke to him. For hours. Cried over him. Cuddled him. Told him everything we wished we had told him more often when he was with us. Thinking of the many things we did not get to say. We recounted every memory, adventure, and the fabulous journey we had shared. He was sleeping. It was just like he was sleeping. He was so beautiful. So completely at peace. My beautiful boy.

We took the time to touch every single part of his body. To stroke every single fibre of fur between our fingers, lift and feel his floppy ears, and hold his massive paws. I closed my eyes and smelled him. I tried to imprint on my brain every ounce of him, to cherish him so I could forever close my eyes and remember everything about him. Every feeling, every sense, every memory.

The family came up to say their goodbyes. To thank him. To tell him how much they loved him. My mum shed tears and told him he was the best boy. My father, who was not one to show his emotions, was blubbering away at the loss of his big friend. This was the first and only time I could remember witnessing my dad cry. I was told the French sometimes refer to dogs as 'Beasts of Sorrow', predeceasing us and inflicting the suffering of loss upon us. In the end, 'you will discover how much you care, and you give your heart to a dog to tear.'[3]

We buried Bert in the garden. In his garden. Where he used to sit and sniff the air and watch his kingdom. Where he sat and crunched carrots. Where he used to sit and watch mum and dad do the gardening and refuse to move when we needed to cut the grass. Where he lay in the sun and snored. He will forever be right outside our doors so we can speak to him, see him and be with him every day. It will forever be Bert's Garden.

My brother Scott and I laboriously dug throughout the day. We battled through layers of chalk and rock for hours to ensure we had a deep and suitable resting place for a special boy. It was a race against the light before it got dark. Bert was placed on his comfortable, memory foam bed with several quilted duvets to keep him warm. He was positioned carefully to ensure he was looking towards the house to see us. Everyone took turns to say some words, a goodbye, in his honour. A box of treats, chews and special mementos were placed by his side for when he wakes up; obviously hungry after his big journey.

As we said our goodbye, the stars shone brightly, and he glistened under the light of the moon. It felt dignified and worthy of one so deserving.

I will never know Bert's exact birthdate. However, from our estimates, he spent 3795 days on this earth, 2741 days by my side. His only fault – he did not live long enough. Days, weeks, years; don't they go by in a blink. He spent only two days of those 2741 without me, Dawn, or one of our family who loved him. His final two days. That may be my only regret with the clarity of hindsight. I do not regret my decision to let him go. Of course, scenarios go around in my head; what if we had done this or that? However, I know, and it helps me find peace, that every decision we made in his life was out of love and what we felt was best for him at the time. A small part of the loss is living with the ever-lasting doubt, the unknown we can never prove or disprove. Truth can be a weapon, but truth can also be closure. The unknown doubt will always dig away on the worst days. Would I have started hydrotherapy earlier? Yes. Would I have put him on a diet earlier or not given him that digestive biscuit? Of course. Hindsight.

But if I look back, Bert was truly happy. Bert loved us, and he knew we loved him. It was a mutual agreement. He had a great life. I would not have changed much at all about our time together except not being with him his final two nights; I wish I had been there. I wish I had cradled, kissed, and reassured him those nights. No one should ever be left alone in their old age, especially during their final days. I get emotional when I think, what if he thought we had abandoned him, like at the beginning of his life, when he needed us the most? I wish I had kept him home and given him a glorious, final swansong. A fitting farewell; a dip in the loch and the last supper feast.

I am not religious, but I have faith. A faith in something greater for him and that I will get to see him again one day. I believe heaven may not be exactly how you want it to be but what you need it to be. My only prayers, or words, I say to the stars at night, are: I love you, I miss you, and I truly hope you know we never abandoned you. We were trying to help you. We were trying to save you so we could have even longer together. I hope he knows. I am sure he knows. Those 2741 days of pure love and devotion were enough to let him know – mum and dad would not do that. He knew he was our world.

Every dog owner always wants more time. There is no escaping their premature mortality. I have come to realise that meeting him earlier or Bert living longer would not change that. I would still want more time and think it wasn't long enough. Cherish every day, every walk, every kiss, every time they wake you up during the night or interrupt you when you are 'too busy'. One day you would give anything to have a tiny slice of it just one more time.

I reflect on the days I complained of boredom or stayed watching television with time on my hands. There were days I was tired and put off going on new, exciting adventures with Bert. Time stands still, and we can do it tomorrow. Then one day, we are blindsided, realising we do not have any more time, our future has ceased to exist, and our time together has become our past. The days and places which we once treasured become only memories. We only appreciate time when it becomes too late.

And now Bert is dead. Nature is brutal and tells the truth as it is. He is no longer physically with me. Death is an uncomfortable subject, and we prefer euphemisms to protect us and make life tolerable. In China, souls traditionally ride on a crane to a Western Paradise. For some Native Americans, the spirit goes to Wakan

Tanka, a paradise in the sky, where they are free from all pain and suffering. But for dog lovers, the passage to the afterlife is over the Rainbow Bridge. Like Norse mythology and the Bifrost Bridge, a rainbow gateway which transports between earth and the gods. The Rainbow Bridge is a beautiful place which returns our pets to health and vigour. Dogs live a loyal and faithful life so there is no need for redemptions – except for stealing a few gammon rolls. They are content and happy, running and playing. Just as we remember them in our dreams and memories.

Until one day, Bert suddenly stops frolicking with friends in the green meadows and stares intently into the distance with his bright brown eyes. He breaks off from the group and sets off across the green with the speed of his youth. The pads of his feet barely touch the ground as he glides, gathering speed and momentum.

He has spotted us. On that day, we will meet in a joyous reunion; never to be parted again.

PRECIOUS FINAL FEW DAYS

# GOODBYE FOR NOW

# 7. Legacy

But the story doesn't end, as I've never really gone
Just resting in the garden and life must still go on
It's a truly special place, where I am laid to rest
You said I did deserve it as I simply was THE BEST!

I love my water feature and the bench where mum can sit
To share some special moments – as we chat a little bit
The gentle running water reminds me of those days
Plopping in the rivers in my own peculiar way.

As she sits upon the bench, a robin comes along
He sits upon my wall and sings a lovely song
I'm sure mum knows the meaning when a robin does appear
I'm sending her a sign to show that I am near.

BERT

## Anderson Graham

I have a special thank you for my lovely caring mum
I know about the 'stones' and everything you've done
To keep me in your heart – so I hope that you believe
That is where I'll stay as I don't intend to leave!

All around the world, my tribute stones appear
On mountain tops, parks and lakes, in countries far and near
America, Australia, South Africa – the lot
So proud my name lives on. Forgotten, I am not.

Every day you talk to me, sending all your love
A big smile on my face as I watch you from above
My life was really magic, and if life was truly fair
Every dog would get the chance to live like Bert the Bear!

Now you wake up each morning, searching for my touch
I still hear you whisper, "I love you oh so much"
There's nights when you reach out and try to stroke my hair
Although you cannot feel me, be sure I'm always there.

And now I'm really happy to see you smile once more
With Albert and wee Bera, you're a family of four!
The pair of them look lively. They'll keep you on your toes
Not quite as chilled as me but then again, who knows?

Maybe in the future, they will learn to plod and plop
But I wouldn't hold my breath cos they never seem to stop!
Perhaps you could remind them, in everything they do
They better not forget... Big Brother's watching you!!!

Albert, he's like me, he's such a gentle soul
Bera has my appetite – she fairly clears the bowl
My lovely home is once again a place so filled with joy
But I'll NEVER understand why they chase a squeaky toy!

So, I haven't really left you. I'm with you every day
Always close beside you all – just a breath away
And when you see a rainbow or a little dancing 'ball'
That's my sign to let you know, I'm here to guide you all.

And many years from now, when it's time for you 'to go'
There's something I must tell you. I'm not sure if you know
But there's a Rainbow Bridge, and that is where we'll meet
Just make sure you remember to bring along a treat!

We frolic through the meadows – yes dad, I can run!
There's no such thing as calories. I can eat for fun
I've met some Twitter pals, and Buster lives quite near
Please, just keep on smiling cause it's 'heavenly' up here.

Keep going on adventures, make memories anew
Let other pups experience the love I shared with you
If ever you feel sad, remember what they say
I'll be waiting at The Bridge till we meet again one day!

# Chapter Seven: Legacy

Bert's story did not end there.

The next day the sun rose again, and the world went on, but I was left with only emptiness and memories. The days, weeks and months which followed Bert's passing were the worst I have ever had the misfortune of experiencing. My dream home became only a house, devoid of all the smiles, joy and love we had come to expect. For eight years, my morning routine was going out, starting the day with fresh air, and making memories with Bert. It was always an instant dopamine boost to start the day. I had lost that. Dark was the day. I was waking up sluggish and going to work without happiness. I returned from work without a purpose. No routine. No one waiting for me, to greet me with a wagging tail or give me a hero's welcome on my return. The whimper of our welcome was silenced. Quiet is not always peaceful, and the echo of silence is torture. I would find myself going to bed by 5pm, not knowing what to do with myself. The earlier I fell asleep, the sooner I got to dream.

Dreaming helped me remember. Close my eyes and live those days again. I hope he is as happy as he is in my dreams. That large goofy smile. I often dreamed I cradled him in my arms. No fancy trips to far-off destinations or adventures, just together. Awakening to reality at the start was a continuous dagger blow to the heart.

The myriad of memories and endless moments make up a life. We cherished each and every memory. Those memories may have passed, but if you take care to hold them in your heart, they will always last. Memories have the immeasurable power to make us happy, whilst at the same time turning even our brightest day dark. But memories and dreams allowed me to see him; that was all I needed.

Life is less about things we gather and more about who we have loved, and who loved us in return. It is less about where you have been and more about who you lived that life with. If we do it correctly, the relationships we make in life already place us in heaven.

'If there's another world, he lived in bliss;
If there is none, he made the best of this.'[1]

I found those days extremely bleak, lonely, and difficult. Dawn was not ready to talk about her boy openly. It was far too raw and far too painful. If I am honest, what kept me going and brought me so much warmth was Twitter. People's kind and thoughtful words about Bert made my heart swell with pride. From all corners of the globe, I was receiving messages telling me how Bert was the first thing they would look for each morning or how much solace they found in watching Bert living life at his own pace. Bert was a companion to many, especially during the difficult lockdown period. He created friendships through a common love for amazing dogs; small, large, young, old, or no longer with us. He never did anything most other older dogs across the world wouldn't or couldn't do, but people appeared to relate to Bert. A dog with grit, perseverance and enjoying the simple pleasure of living. I had messages from people who told me they had never commented on any posts but wanted to let me know how Bert really helped them smile through their troubles. People resonated with him. In so many ways, he could be referred to as an unremarkable dog, but everyone seemed to realise that this unremarkable dog, living his life with simple pleasures and joy, was truly remarkable.

I will never be able to express how grateful I was to receive those messages. The pride I felt was indescribable. However, I had a shallow fear. I knew how many people cared for Bert, expressed considerate words, and were upset by his passing. However, I also know the reality of social media. It is a dog they had never met. It would have been easy for them to see Bert's terrible news, move on to the next post, and get on with their everyday lives. Clarifying that people loved and cared for him and that his life mattered to others was a much-needed solace. Perhaps I should not have needed that assurance, but I did. Thank you.

We received cards, many still on display two years later, expressing the most thoughtful words. We received packages of mementos to help us remember Bert. A commissioned teddy bear of Bert, which will forever take pride of place on the bookcase overlooking where we spend most of our evenings together. A painting of Bert surrounded by his favourite bluebells, and even personalised stamps of his beautiful face, which will NEVER be sent.

When you lose a dog, you quickly discover who are and are not dog people. I admit to feeling resentment towards people who just did not get it. Worse if they did not even acknowledge it. In hindsight, I know some people just don't know what to say or how to approach the situation of loss. I appreciated and was forever thankful to the people who paid their condolences. The acknowledgement of knowing how important he was to us. For some, it was words, telling us they know exactly how we feel, and it was clear that they sadly do, and others just a glance or nod to express their compassion. At work, I was an open book. I told pupils what had happened. I openly burst into tears in front of classes. The pupils were exceptional. They were more open than the adults. They drew cards, said sorry, and were incredibly respectful of my feelings. I walked into a classroom, and a younger pupil blurted out, "your dog died". There is a charm in children who just express what's on their minds, without malice, and it was the first time I had laughed since the incident. A parent stopped me one morning to thank me for being so open with my emotions. She said it was important for her son to see a male role model express their emotions. She told me the boy's grandparent had passed away, but he did not show any emotions until he came home from school that day, and he let his feelings out and cried to his mum. That meant a lot to me.

There was a day at work when I was about to break down. I was struggling. My mind could not concentrate and I was becoming increasingly crabbit[2]. A colleague, a caring friend, walked past me and just gave me the faintest touch on the shoulder, asking if I was okay. They cuddled me, and I remember just holding on so tightly. Some days were harder than others. Some days I needed that. Some days I wanted to tell everyone and anyone all about him, and other days I wanted to be left completely alone. Some days it helped me, and some days it hurt so much. It was always bittersweet.

Shortly after Bert passed, I went to the toilet in the middle of the night. I never put the lights on. The route is automated. In the hallway, on the way back to the bedroom, I felt what I can only describe as a wagging tail striking against my knee. I put the light on, and there was nothing there – an empty hallway. I felt a huge sigh of relief at that moment. He was still here. He had not left me. He knew how much I still needed him by my side. I was not ready to live my life without his presence. I went to bed with a tear in my eye but a smile on my face. Ever since that night, I lean over to Bert's bed, which remains at the side of our bed, and dangle my hand to wish him goodnight. I dangle out a hand to pat his head. Just in case.

I miss that reassuring touch.

'A dog is the only thing on earth that loves you more than he loves himself.' I strongly disagree. From my experience, dog lovers also fit that category. I, without doubt, loved Bert more than I loved myself. I would gladly have swapped places with him, without a moment's hesitation, to have him healthy and happy again.

We instantly turned our home into a shrine. The porch is full of Bert art pieces we had collected over the years – our way of feeling we are greeted by him every time we return to the house. His collar takes its rightful place above the doorway of his forever home. His handsome face appears in photos throughout the house. His drying robe remains on his peg.

Memorialisation is powerful, healthy and helps with the healing process. It helps me to relive those many years of many happy memories, shifting the focus from the loss. A way to celebrate and prevent us from being stuck in that overwhelming tidal wave of misery. A place to be with them in spirit.

The garden was selected as the location of Bert's memorial. We got in touch with a highly skilled and well-recommended mason to discuss potential ideas. Alain came over to meet us, and we told him our story, Bert's story, and how we needed Bert's Garden to be beautiful; somewhere where we could sit, be with him, talk to him, and always be near him. Our discussion was in-depth, with him revealing he also had two Labradors, who were his world. Alain walking away, unaware we were still looking, stopped at Bert's graveside and threw a dog biscuit on top. Dawn and I knew he was the one.

Bert passed in September, and work for the garden would begin over winter. Not ideal for paving, deliveries, or general outdoor work, but Alain was perfect. He created a space which we are proud of and which honours Bert. There is a large stone, rustic wall above where Bert used to lay and eat his carrots or bask in the sun (when it made its rare appearance in Scotland). To sit with our boy, two elm wood benches were integrated into the wall, with natural lines that change colour throughout the seasons. Separating the benches is a central stone partition which displayed a beautiful slate memorial stone which read 'Bert – 10.5.10 – 29.9.20'. The whole area was slabbed and in the centre was a stone plinth supporting a prominent, sphere water feature that softly ran down into the pebbles below. This symbolised Bert's love for slow, flowing water. It was all finished off with native shrubs around the edges. This was our special place.

'If I had a flower for every time I thought of you, I could walk through my garden forever.'[3]

We worked hard to keep the garden colourful and attractive. The natural beauty of a garden can be like a small piece of heaven. We planted roses, sunshine yellow, to represent Bert's golden glow.

Every morning we go outside to greet our boy. Last thing at night, before going to bed, we wish him goodnight, tell him we love him and ask him to come and join us. Dawn frequently goes out alone, with a coffee and just sits there. She finds it spiritual. Peaceful. So very Bert.

Talking to Bert has remained an essential part of our lives. Whether it is a 'good morning' or seeking spiritual guidance, it remains vital in our grieving process.

Scotland has the legendary tale of Greyfriars Bobby, the Skye Terrier, who displayed faithful loyalty by sitting on his departed master's grave every day for twelve years. As simple, inferior humans, we cannot match a dog for loyalty, but we can echo the sentiment. Every morning, every time we leave the house, or every evening.

At night, under the galaxy of stars, we hold each other under the light of the moon and look at the stars above. We search for the brightest star in the sky – that's Bert. Bert is a supernova. A supernova is a dead star, yet it is the most beautiful specimen in the universe. It outshines entire galaxies, radiating more energy than our sun will in its entire lifetime. When it reaches the end of its life, it explodes in a brilliant burst of light. He still shines so brightly – however, I cannot justify the radiating energy part when it comes to Bert.

Fate works in funny and mysterious ways. If we had not discovered Twitter. If timings did not align. Sadly, if Bert had not passed.

Approximately ten days after Bert passed away, I received a message. It was from someone who followed Bert's journey and wished to pass on their condolences. However, their follow-up message began, "I know it's far too soon, but...". George told me he lived reasonably local, and his beautiful black Labrador had recently had a litter of puppies. Out of the nine, there was only one golden male Labrador. He told me how much he loved Bert's posts, and knowing how loved, how great a life Bert had, he would be honoured if we would be interested. It was far too soon. We had not grieved. I told Dawn. We dismissed it. However, the topic kept resurfacing in daily conversations. We agreed that we should at least ask some questions.

The puppy was born Saturday evening, the final moments of the 26th of September 2020. The same Saturday evening that Bert took his final steps at home. I like to think Bert knew his old body was sore and failing him, so he transferred his soul and health into his new fresh body to continue his adventures with us. As soon as I had convinced myself of this story, there was clear temptation.

My fear had always been moving on too soon. Disrespecting Bert by 'replacing' him. He was the love of my life. Luckily, someone said to me that it would be great to give another dog the love and quality of life Bert had received. They said, "Bert taught you how to love. It would be more insulting if you did not use what he taught you. He would want you to love again."

I spoke to my mother, expecting her to tell me off for even considering this so soon, but she asked me one question.

"How would you feel if you didn't take the dog?"

We arranged to go and visit the puppies. They were adorable. I had never owned a puppy before, so I was naively unaware of just how razor-sharp those teeth were. We sat on the floor, observing the nine tiny Labrador puppies taking turns waking up and stumbling over each other. There were six black puppies, the same as their mother, Bella, one red fox-like their father, Teale, and two golden. A few were lifted out of the pen, progressing to climb and clamber over us with squeals of delight and mischievous curiosity. Despite my fingers, ears, nose, and chin being bitten as I lifted the squirming little ball of fur – at one point dangling from my beard – we fell in love. It was the first time we had both managed to laugh and smile. It was an immediate decision. As soon as we walked in and Dawn set eyes on the puppies, I knew the discussion beforehand to not be too impulsive was gone. That ship had sailed. To be honest, I would have taken any of them, but as soon as we knew which one was earmarked for us, I could not take my eyes off him. We agreed, there and then, to take the puppy.

The only way to be happy is to love.

'In my end is my beginning.'[4] Bert's death is spiritually intertwined with a new cycle, new life, and a new beginning. This was the beginning of Bert's legacy. Before I met Bert, I could not quite imagine what living with a dog might be like. After his passing, I could not imagine any other way.

We knew we wanted to incorporate Bert into the name. With Bert in his name, it would be impossible for him to be anything but the best of dogs. It would be impossible for us to say the name and not instantly think of his predecessor. The bonus was that when we met the young pup, he was the chunkiest of the litter – perfect. The name would fit. Albert would be joining our family.

At this point, I want to mention the elephant in the room – ADOPT, DON'T SHOP. A lot of people fell in love with Bert because of his character but also due to his rags-to-riches tale. A dog wandering the street, finding eternal love and happiness. Dawn and I used to volunteer at a local dog rescue centre. At the weekends, I would walk Bert in the morning and whilst he took his rest, we would pop to the centre to walk a few of the dogs in the shelter. We loved it. At one point, we grew attached to a troubled little Collie from Romania. She was aggressive and anxious. But she was also incredibly gorgeous. Every week I would ask if I could walk Lily. At first, they were reluctant as she was 'troubled', but they knew it was her I wanted to walk and my reason for attending, so over time, I could take her out more and more. We grew a bond. She, like every dog, only wanted to be loved but took longer than some to trust and accept that love.

We used to walk around a neighbouring golf course, and if she got an old, wooden golf tee in her mouth, I could not get it out without a snarl or a bite. Lily's issue was she was protective of her food. She had grown up in an environment locked in a small cage with many other dogs, where she learned to fend for herself and protect food at all costs. Literally, a dog-eat-dog environment. However, gradually, she would lick me and roll onto her back for tickles. A barrier had been broken down, and trust was forming. Due to Bert's age and having grown accustomed to his slow and peaceful life, we wouldn't rehome another dog for fear it would alter his confidence or happiness. We did discuss the idea of fostering Lily to help her grow to find her forever home. Bert and Lily had been on several walks and walked contently together. We had someone come out and assess our environment. At this time, we were told we wouldn't be considered for foster or rehoming due to us being full-time workers. We also looked into registering interest with a local Labrador charity, but the waiting list was years. Adoption is a wonderful way to rehome a dog who will be more appreciative and show you more love than you could ever hope. Sadly, it does not work for every family and every household.

On the 20th of November 2020, only fifty-two days since we lost our beloved Bert, we welcomed home Albert. This was much quicker than we would ever have planned. However, those fifty-two days were torture. It was too long to be without a dog and everything they bring to a home. I had no purpose. No routine. We were so excited to take Albert home but also terrified.

Firstly, we were worried because we had never had a puppy before. You can read as many books, watch online videos, and speak to as many people as you like, but nothing can prepare you for the reality of the chaos we were about to behold. However, secondly, and more importantly, we were terrified that we were replacing our boy. Never. A new dog never replaces or makes you forget the previous dog. Albert was just the next chapter in Bert's story.

Albert was the last of the nine puppies to be collected. I cannot imagine what that day would be like for a young puppy. His sole experience of sleep had been warmly nestled under, on top or against his warm siblings, and one by one, they vanished. Wrapped in a blanket, engulfed in the scent of his siblings, Albert was gently carried outside to the car. Dawn sat in the back seat, comforting, and holding baby Albert all the way home.

With a new dog comes the opportunity to set new lifelong rules and routines. I told Dawn we would need to initially sleep him in a crate until he was toilet trained. I put the crate beside the bed with his blanket and cuddly sheep toy. We had left the sheep with the puppies weeks previous; to play with so that Albert would have a familiar toy, but also that it was smothered in the smell of his siblings and Bella. It contained a beating heart mechanism to replicate his mother to help him settle those first few nights. Albert was placed inside. I brushed my teeth and returned to the bedroom to see Albert snuggled between the cushions and the headrest, sound asleep. "But he was crying." And from that day onwards, he never slept anywhere else.

Albert was precious. He was cuddly and adorable and, at points, an absolute terror. Like any puppy, or so I'm told. That was my fault. I played rough and tumble with him, as I did with Bert, forgetting that this young puppy did not have an off switch. He did not stop until he had a mouthful of my jumper, shorts, or fingers. Several items of clothes were kept solely for puppy play and were torn to shreds. Razor sharp puppy teeth tested the resolve and quality of tables, chairs, carpets, and walls. However, he picked up simple commands quickly, and even though sleep-deprived chaos was now our lives, he was a very good boy.

Initially, Albert wasn't allowed to walk far. We stuck with the '5-minute rule' to minimise his walks and for his long-term health. He got a taster of the farm, every day smelling the aromas without being set free to fully explore. It was a while before we ventured on 'Bert's walks'. I remember the first morning we made it all the way to the river where Bert used to lie and just enjoy the flowing, icy water in a totally peaceful state. I broke down in tears. I felt incredibly guilty. Albert was staying by my side, working on his heel work, when a song – on shuffle, on a random playlist – came through my headphones. I had never heard the song before, and I have not since. I do not know what the song was. But I remember the chorus.

'I'm running now. I'm running now.'

I needed to hear that. It felt like a verification that I had Bert's approval. Quickly, my guilt turned to relief, and I looked up and smiled, still with tears streaming down my face.

Albert was the best decision we ever could have made. He brought smiles and laughter back into our home. He was proof that the heart is never full; it can always expand and make room for you to love again. Grief is only love with nowhere to go. Now we had somewhere to channel that love and give another dog a wonderful life.

Instead of replacing him, Albert enhances our memories of Bert. Watching him on walks would bring memories flooding back and the capacity to let us enjoy the moment even more. Albert is fast, agile, and slim. Bert was none of those. Albert becomes obsessive when chasing a ball or stick. For him, it's the greatest day ever anytime a ball appears from the pocket. On a walk, he will never stop to take a break or just take in the moment. However, no matter their unique and distinctive characteristics, there are so many similarities to make us feel he is guided by someone with experience and knowledge. Like Bert, he loves to snuggle on the sofa with his mummy when he is tired. He's a gentle giant, and as much as he loves playing with other dogs, he would always prefer to be right by your side, just like Bert. And he loves his food. Just like... well, every Labrador, actually.

One day, Dawn began drawing. Grieving sparked her creative side. Sketching Bert helped her come to terms with him not being here but still allowed her to see him anytime she wished. She then began to design memorial stones for her boy. She made a big batch. We would pick up large, round, and smooth pebbles from the river at the bottom of the farm, dry them and then she would use acrylic paint to design them and leave messages before covering them in a sealant to protect them from the wet, Scottish elements.

We began retracing our steps from Bert's favourite walks around our home and back to where we previously lived. We found quiet, peaceful spots off the beaten track and placed a stone. It was highly therapeutic. He would forever, or at least a while, be in some of his favourite spots. These included the top of hills from his younger days, at the side of rivers and wedged into stone walls on hikes. We shared pictures on Twitter of a few of the stones being placed, and were overwhelmed by the response.

Soon, some of Bert's friends took it further and paid homage. In far-flung corners of the world, a stone with Bert's name sits in many beautiful spots. From the top of Table Mountain overlooking Cape Town, South Africa, to the base of the Rocky Mountains in Canada, to Skopje, the capital of North Macedonia. To think our boy travelled and gets to see the world from these captivating spots is heart-warming. I'm envious. More importantly, I'm thankful.

And then along came Bera. The younger sister of Albert, sharing the same birth parents. We kept in touch with the first litter families and organised their first birthday party at the beach. Through these chats, we discovered Albert's mum Bella, was having another litter with Albert's dad, Teale. Albert, our little angel, had been a delight, with a few usual puppy terrors included, but we had no doubt we wanted to do it again. Dogs are pack animals and may enjoy the company and companionship of their own kind. We were warned that we should wait a few years between the dogs. However, we decided two puppies, from the same parents, of similar age growing up and playing together, was too big an opportunity not to accept.

It was not until after the birth, until just before we went to view the puppies, that we decided on a boy or a girl. We were changing our minds frequently between gender and colour. Do we get two boys, risk the potential fight for male dominance or a girl, and deal with the issues that obviously entails? Do we go golden and continue the legacy, or do we go for a black Labrador? We changed our minds at the last moment. Thankfully, another family were happy to accept the change before anyone went to collect a puppy. We went for a girl. Our first girl. Our dog walker, Juliet, did try to warn us that girls are usually feistier – she was not wrong.

Whichever dog you are lucky enough to take home very quickly becomes the only dog you were ever meant to spend your life with. I would have loved and cherished any of those puppies, but she was meant to be with us.

Bera, as a girl's name, is of Teutonic origin, and the meaning is 'bear'. Again, we wanted to have a link to Bert, as this will always be part of his legacy. However, it was also in celebration of their mother, Bella. She has bestowed upon us the honour of loving two of her precious babies. In fact, both golden puppies have black fur spots on their nose to represent their beautiful biological mother.

Albert and Bera are best friends. And like best friends and siblings, they terrorise each other as much as they love each other. Well, she terrorises, he tolerates. Albert welcomed the fragile little puppy, moving gingerly in her presence. Bera did not return the favour and would instigate carnage and chaos. He attempted to ignore her advances, but she persevered. Barking and taunting, yipping, and bouncing. Frustrated by his lack of playfulness, she would pounce on him and force his hand to a battle. She would go for the drooping ears or slide underneath and nip at the legs. We tried to allow natural socialisation and pecking order to take its course. Like his big brother Bert, Albert was too gentle and sweet to put her in her place. Occasionally I would have to risk life and limb, and stop the rammy[5]. After each encounter, they would snuggle into each other and never wish to be apart. Although Albert was wise enough to always keep one eye open, awaiting the next attack!

They play chase with purpose around Bert's memorial in all weathers. His beautiful grass garden is now a dirt track with its own alarm system. Nobody will walk past our hedge without anyone in the vicinity knowing someone is here, and they are not welcome. But our large garden would be wasted and empty without my dogs, even if a few trees and shrubs are sacrificed for their chewy sticks. It's a place where people smile, and dogs are happy – a fitting memorial to Bert.

They have their routines for walking. Albert always needs to be on the outside, ever so slightly ahead, with Bera wedged between us both in the middle. Their favourite destination, like Bert's, is the water. You may not be able to teach an old dog new tricks – but an old dog can teach a young dog new tricks. Passing down wisdom to the next generation. Albert, like Bert, would only tip his toes into the shallow edges, hopelessly gazing out, but did not have that courage to take the plunge. It wasn't until a visit from Alfie, now an older chap, that he watched a master at work.

Alfie raced into the depths, and Albert had the faith to follow the savvy, senior leader. From that moment onwards, his life changed forever. Alfie effortlessly glided through the water with elegance. Albert thrashed, splished, and splashed in fear or hope, trying to stay afloat. His eyes were wide with sheer panic as he stretched for the shore and scrambled back to safety. The next ball was thrown back into the water – Albert followed. Each time with more confidence and increased technique. Alfie beat the young pretender to the ball each time, not yet ready to give up his throne. There was life in the old dog yet. However, there was one effort out in the middle of the water. Albert doubted his own abilities and clambered onto old Alfie, repeatedly dunking his head under the pond, using him as a lifeboat. Was he panicked, or was he trying to eliminate the competition? Albert then passed on his water-seeking skills to Bera. Now no walk is ever complete without an opportunity to run, dive and crash into the waves or if all else fails, a muddy ditch. Bert would be bewildered.

They both have their own personalities, but they complement each other well. They are so different from Bert that we cannot compare, which is a blessing. I think he would be looking down from the Rainbow Bridge, shaking his head in disbelief at the carnage that now beholds his once peaceful abode.

We learned through the mistakes we made with Bert. He was so happy, so loved, but we made mistakes. Albert and Bera's diets have been extremely healthy. A lot of fruit and vegetables, food weighed out, certainly no milk each day, and, as much as possible, no human 'titbits' (or tidbits to my American friends). They are healthy, fit, and svelte dogs. We cannot predict the future, but if we can minimise the chance of osteoarthritis, which shortened our boy's life, we will do all we can. And of course, they do love a big, crunchy carrot. Some things will never change.

There are nights when I think I feel Bert the most. In the dark of the night, I lie in bed and stroke my dogs whilst I'm asleep, and as I awake, I just feel the weight on my chest or a fistful of hair in my hands, and for a moment, I still think it's Bert. I'm never disappointed to discover it's Albert or Bera, but for those few seconds, my boy is still with me. I don't allow my eyes to adjust. I allow myself to dream and imagine. I still hold on to the dream that one day Bert will come and walk with me and brush against my hand. But at night, I sleep beside my dogs. All three of them.

You can love a dog so much, but you can never love them as much as you will miss them. I loved that boy with all my heart, but the heartache and pain I experienced when I lost him was like no other. Be brave; allow yourself to see the sunlight and love again after suffering through the dark storm. It's remarkable how resolute the heart is, to be broken into a million pieces, yet allow us to love again – and then some.

I am so glad we opened our home to Albert and Bera. They have been a pleasure to love and to watch them grow and develop into such wonderful dogs. I am so proud of them, and Bert would be proud of them too.

Every time we walk past Bert's tree, up a hill, or by a river and see his memorial stone, we kiss it and remember him. Whenever an item of clothing is missing, I think of when Bert stole our clothes for his comfort. Whenever I hear the crunch of a carrot, see an older dog plod, or hear loud, foghorn snoring – I think of Bert.

Bert was always a great dog. A best friend. When you lose someone you love, they never really leave you. They will always be in your heart. He will be with us everywhere. Forever missed and forever remembered, but mostly forever loved.

I will always remember that every good thing in my life started when I met a dog called Bert.

BERT'S MEMORIAL GARDEN

# MEMORIAL STONES

HE FOUND MY SMILE AGAIN

PRINCE ALBERT

# REGAL AND HANDSOME

PRINCESS BERA

THE MOST BEAUTIFUL GIRL IN THE WORLD

I LOVE MY BROTHER
I TOLERATE MY SISTER

SIBLINGS
YOU ARE ALWAYS BY MY SIDE

BERT FOREVER AND ALWAYS

# Epilogue

In the end, we are our stories.

Unfortunately, our heroes do not always make it to the end of the story. However, the stories we share keep our loved ones alive when they can no longer tell their own tale. By sharing their stories, and our memories of them, we keep their names and story timeless. Bert's life is celebrated through his stories, but no story lives on unless someone wants to listen and hear it. I am so grateful to you for being his audience. His life now extends much further than his adventures with me.

Bert's story is our story, but in sharing it with others, I have come to realise that, in reality, it is the story of anyone and everyone who has had the pleasure of loving and the heartache of losing a dog.

I began writing this book one year after Bert's passing. I found the process therapeutic but emotionally draining. I found it difficult when I could not remember every tiny detail of his life when I was re-telling his tale. During an emotional moment, struggling with the guilt that memories were fading and scared I was forgetting him, Dawn told me, "You may forget things you said to him. You may forget the moments you spent with him. But you will never forget how Bert made you feel."

I have not and will never forget how Bert made me feel.

# Notes

## 1. Fate

1. SSPCA – Scottish Society for Prevention of Cruelty to Animals

## Chapter One: Fate

1. Roger Grenier, *The Difficulty of Being a Dog*, "Our Great Men" (2000)
2. Oscar Wilde, *Lady Windermere's Fan* (1892)

## Chapter Two: New Beginnings

1. Den – Scots word meaning wooden glen
2. Poohsticks – First mentioned in *The House at Pooh Corner* (A.A. Milne, 1928)
3. Dook – To dip or plunge
4. 'Thy glorious, youthful prime' (Robert Burns, 'Man Was Made To Mourn', 1784)
5. Stramash – Fight, an uproar
6. 'Glasgow Kiss' – Headbutt to the face

## Chapter Three: A Mother's Love

1. Dreich – Dreary day with clouds and rain
2. Stoating – Bouncing
3. Drookit – Extremely wet, drenched, from an Old Norse word meaning drowned
4. Alexandra Horowitz, *Being a Dog: Following the Dog into a World of Smell* (2016)
5. Sarah Knapton, the *Telegraph*, 'Feeling stressed? Sniff your partner's jumper to calm down, say scientists' (5th January 2018)

## 4. New Home. New Adventures

1. Flit – To move house

## Chapter Four: New Home. New Adventures

1. *Historical Thesaurus of Scots* (2015)

## Chapter Five: An Older Gentleman

1. Trootling – Walking slowly and reluctantly
2. Bahookie – The buttocks
3. Nuddle – To walk quickly with head bent forward
4. Taps aff – (Scots Vernacular) Literally 'tops off'. The removal of one's shirt in the event of warm weather. A phenomenon rarely seen in Glasgow
5. Overmorrow – The day after tomorrow

## Chapter Six: Goodbye for Now

1. Respair – Recovery from despair
2. F. Scott Fitzgerald – *The Great Gatsby* (1925)
3. Rudyard Kipling – 'The Power of the Dog' (1922)

## Chapter Seven: Legacy

1. Robert Burns – 'Epitaph on a Friend'
2. Crabbit – Ill-tempered
3. Alfred Lord Tennyson
4. T.S. Eliot, 'Four Quartets'
5. Rammy – Quarrel or brawl

# Acknowledgments

This book is the culmination of the social media platform Twitter. The story is ours. Everything else to do with the creation of this book is due to the support of friends worldwide.

Thousands of people encouraged me to write the book. Many more cared for Bert and continue to do so. For that, I will be forever thankful.

A few people stand out as having made this book possible.

My mother, who wrote Bert's poem, telling his life story, encouraged me, and motivated me to expand and put the words down on paper. She is my creative muse and inspiration when it comes to telling tales. She has always been there for me and would support me in any endeavour I wish to partake in.

My father, whose judgment I trust more than anyone else. Going over the text with a fine-tooth comb – if there's a mistake, blame him! As a child playing football, my dad was the only person I asked how I played. He was honest and never over-praised, so to hear him say the book was "excellent" was the clarification I needed.

Dawn, my partner, cried every time I read her a passage, letting me know I was on the right track. Thank you for not complaining about how much time and dedication I was spending on this project – you knew it was all in our boy's name, and it had to be perfect. However, it would have been finished six months earlier if you had walked the dogs a bit more often and let me get on!

Albert and Bera for patiently waiting for their walks and dindins until I finished a paragraph, a page, or a chapter. Revisiting Bert's favourite spots with you helped me relive memories – although some experiences were at a vastly different pace. You rescued me from grief and allowed me to write with a smile on my face as you snuggled into my feet.

My 'Beta Readers' and editors. For turning my amateur work into something of which I am proud. Lori Kuhn-Hancock for editing my grammar throughout the process. Deborah Powell, my reality check, told me it was not ready and prevented me from rushing its release. My Norden queens, Hilkka Olkinuora and Maria Stefansdottir Bernsden ensured the book translated successfully. Most importantly, Bangsi, who snuggled into his mum Maria and kept a watchful eye throughout the whole process.

John Heim. Your illustrations bring the poem to life, adding wit with your fabulous sketches.

Laurel Gauthier for ensuring I was never overstretched, and that support was always at hand.

Patricia Veale for offering her time and expertise to ensure you were able to find this book.

Claire Wingfield and Kieran McLoughlin for giving the book its final edit, typeset, and in general, transforming my work from draft to done. For creating a book I am proud to release in Bert's name.

And finally, Bert, for giving me a wonderful life worth sharing.

If you would like to join Bert, Albert, and Bera's adventures, we would be honoured if you followed us on Twitter – @BearBertthe.

Thank you.

Ross Graham

Printed in Great Britain
by Amazon

32363333R00119